Er

Secrets

Master The Secrets Of Social Confidence
And Skilled Relationships Using Speed
Reading, Body Language And The
Psychology Of Human Behavior

—

Including DIY-Exercises

Patrick Lightman

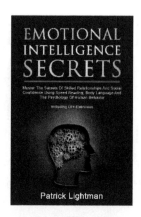

Emotional Intelligence Secrets

Master The Secrets Of Skilled Relationships And Social
Confidence Using Speed Reading, Body Language And The
Psychology Of Human Behavior

Copyright © 2019 by Patrick Lightman

Do you want to step up your People Analysis Skills and jumpstart your Decision-Making Game?

CLICK here to grab your Behavioral Science Cheat Sheet for FREE NOW.

How To Analyze People 1

The #1 Analyst Guide To Human Behavior, Body Language, Personality Types And Effectively Reading People

How To Analyze People 2
Learn Rapid Deduction Techniques To Think And Analyze People Like Sherlock Holmes

How To Analyze People 3
Uncover Sherlock Holmes' Secrets To Analyze Anyone On The Spot
-
Including DIY-Exercises

How To Analyze People 4

Inside The Mind Of A Master Detective. Secret Insights About His Mindset And How He Thinks

-

Including DIY-Exercises

How to Analyze People 1

The #1 Analyst Guide To Human Behavior,
Body Language, Personality Types And
Effectively Reading People

Patrick Lightman

Introduction

If I were to ask you, "What is the single most important skill that will give in an edge over others in a personal, professional and social set-up?", what would your answer be? Think about it carefully. We are social creatures and our ability to succeed in life pretty much depends on our ability to understand people. Throughout our lives, a majority of our time is spend in interaction with people (unless you live in a cardboard box or rabbit hole) and developing new associations. If you were to ask me for the single biggest vital survival and success skill in today's world, it would undoubtedly be the art of analyzing people.

How will you figure out if a prospective employee is a perfect fit for your organizational values and goals? How will you determine if the attractive new lady/man you fancy will be a positive and inspiring long-term mate? How will you identify if a potential client is worth doing business with? How will you cut winsome deals with the right business partners and associates?

How will you forge rewarding business connections at networking events? The master key to all of the above lies in your ability to analyze people, identify their personality, recognize how they think and feel, and above all, communicate in a relevant or appropriate manner based on their personality or behavior.

What is it that primarily drives and motivates people? What is the main personality type? What does their body language reveal about their subconscious thoughts? When you learn to analyze people and identify their fundamental personality type and their thought patterns, you can communicate with them in a more effective and meaningful manner.

When you have the ability to analyze people's behavior and personality, you have an edge when it comes to adapting your own words and actions to develop a winsome rapport with the other person, thus forming more productive and fulfilling interpersonal relationships or professional associations. Well, analyzing people isn't just vital for FBI sleuths but also for regular, everyday people to form more beneficial connections.

Learning to analyze people is one of the most effective and sharpest skills one can develop in today's fast-paced world where there is no escaping the importance of forming new connections and constantly interacting with people in a frenzied pace. The power to tune in to obvious and subtle clues people give out all the time will equip you with the super power to deliver a message more persuasively or convincingly to a person. When you understand how people think and feel, you'll deliver a message in a manner that is suitable for their thought patterns and actions, thus minimizing the chances of misunderstanding.

You will wield greater control over a conversation or enhance your negotiation skills. People who possess the ability to analyze and read others make for more empathetic friends, partners, employer and leaders. You'll be a razor-sharp businessman and negotiator. As a salesperson or business development person, you'll know exactly what your customer or client wants, which will help boost your sales figures. The scope for conflict-ridden situations will reduce when you understand other people's limitations and structure your communication to suit them.

In short, the skill of reading or analyzing people will determine the quality of relationships you enjoy in life. When you master the tips, techniques and strategies for reading people, you know what to look for while attempting to understand them. What are the unspoken things that are given away by their body language? What does their choice of words reveal about people's personality and attitudes? What is their essential character or personality type? How can you tell if someone is telling the truth or resorting to deception? How can you tell if someone is just being themselves or pretending to be something they clearly aren't?

Monthly glossies have done a lot of disservice to the art of analyzing people by reducing it to pop quizzes such as "What your favorite food says about you" or "What does your favorite lipstick shade reveal about your persona?" It isn't as trivial as marketers or glossy editors have us believe. Analyzing people is about delving into people's minds and understanding their words, thoughts, actions and behavior through psychology-driven principles. It is a comprehensive and deep study that has several factors involved.

Much as you'd like to believe, your favorite fragrance doesn't say much about your personality. It can be highly entertaining and addictive but isn't even remotely accurate. To be a star people analyzer, you need plenty of practice, and the ability to decode personalities.

Though this is a highly intensive field of study involving dynamics of psychology, human behavior, social skills and more, in this book I am packing the most concise, practical and actionable tips that will get you started with reading people.

These techniques can be applied just about anywhere, from your workplace to personal relationships to social life. The sky is the limit when you develop the ability to understand people and influence them using this understanding.

According to research, the ability to analyze people can help us predict the outcome of a negotiation correctly in around 80 percent of all instances. Doesn't that give you an edge when it comes to steering a negotiation in the right direction?

However, let's get started with some valuable fundamental people analyzing rules that will help you set you on the path for being an ace people reader.

Humans are invariably wired throughout primitive times to interact with each other via subconscious signals. Sometimes, people may appear to be happy and content on the face of it, but deep inside their subconscious mind they may harbor feelings of resentment, frustration and disappointment. When you learn to watch out for these clues, you can reach out to people more effectively.

What is a person's primary instinct or gut feeling? What we refer to as our gut feeling or instinct is nothing but our ability to latch on to specific clues that a person transmits at a subconscious level.

When a person smiles, our smile muscles are reflexively triggered at a more subconscious level. Therefore when someone smiles at us, we smile instinctively in return. Human brains are created to capture clues that are not apparent to the conscious mind. For instance, think about the time when a person was behaving in a pleasant and positive manner, yet you experienced a strong sense of discomfort while dealing with them. This is because our minds are wired to latch on to subconscious signals.

It may be something about the person's body language, including high blood pressure, faster heart beat, increased palpitations, sweating and more that our mind catches at a more subconscious level that gives us the feeling that something isn't quite right. This explains why sometimes you just don't like some people even when you don't know them well enough to identify their personality.

Chapter 1:

Human Psychology Basics Decoded

If you track the human evolutionary pattern, you will understand that our brains are wired to conduct accurate readings about our thoughts, actions and behavior. In the absence of language in primitive ages, how did human beings communicate with each other? They communicated through the medium of tone, voice, expression, gestures, postures, signs and other non-verbal mediums. This implies that the skill of reading people already exists within us. It simply needs to be fine-tuned at a conscious level to help us form more productive and fulfilling relationships.

Everyone from trial attorneys to detectives to salespersons to employers can use people analyzing skills to their advantage. Did you know that high-end car salespersons are trained to peep inside their prospective customer's cars to understand their customers better and strike a rapport with them through small talk? If a salesperson sees a golf kit in the back seat of the car, they'll start a conversation about how they enjoy playing golf over the weekends or about a recent golf championship.

Then trial attorneys will attempt to decode where the jury is swinging simply by observing non-verbal clues offered by the jurors while witnesses, officials or the defendant is being cross examined in the stands. They will also brief their clients about maintaining a body language that generally gives out a positive overall impression about him or her to jurors. This can mean eliminating all non-verbal clues that reveal deception or trickery.

Also, when you learn to analyze people, you view them in a more objective and non-judgmental manner. You will also learn to pick up on clues that reveal deception or untruthful behavior. Let us take an example where people try to manipulate you or get what they want using false flattery. When you master the art of reading people, you will be able to determine if people truly feel those compliments from within or they are simply resorting to fake flattery to get what they want. This helps you protect yourself against other people's vested interests.

Here are some amazing advantages of being a people analyzer:

- You are able to enjoy more fulfilling and rewarding interpersonal relationships, thus reducing the pain of unsuitable relationships. You don't want to kiss a thousand frogs to find that one prince/princess, do you?

- It saves you the time, energy and effort of eliminating toxic people and dealing with only those who match your own objectives, values and expectations. People who sap your energy can be shown the door.

- The ability to analyze people can save you tons of money and hours by hiring employees that are a right fit for your organization.

- As a partner or employer, you can tell when people are being deceitful in a relationship or during an interview. You can select a long-term partner who matches not just your own personality but also your values, personality, behavioral traits and more. It will help you weed out dates whose objectives and expectations do not match your own.

- Analyzing people makes you a more power-packed leader. You'll understand your team's goals, motivations, triggers and much more, which can be effectively leveraged for optimizing their performance. This may lead to greater productivity and overall job satisfaction. Learning to read people can be your highway to professional success.

- It is a vital skill when it comes to carrying out negotiations and sales deals. When you figure out how a person prospective client, business associate or customer is thinking, it is simpler to divert the negotiation to your advantage. For instance, if the other party's body language and other non-verbal clues communicate that they are happy with the negotiation terms, yet they ask for a better deal, you know you have to stick your ground because they are simply trying their luck now. Once you realize they are already sold, you won't make any further concessions.

- Reading people helps you fine tune your own verbal and non-verbal communication for creating a dazzling first impression. It helps you package yourself exactly as you want to create more beneficial connections and relationships. You can position yourself as a genuine, credible, friendly and authoritative individual based on the situation by sending the right verbal and non-verbal clues.

- Your empathy factor increases, and you are able to understand people or reach out to them in troubled times more effectively to form more productive interpersonal relationships.

- You increase your chances of performing well at job interviews by sending the right verbal and non-verbal signals to recruiters. You know how to create the right impression by communicating the values, characteristics and ideals that are appropriate for a specific organization or role.

- Tuning in to other people's body language and verbal communication skills makes you an effective speaker. When you gather clues for your audience's body language, you know exactly what they are thinking or feeling about what you're saying. Are they bored, inspired or suspicious about what you are saying? Do they disagree with what you are saying? This will help you quickly change and adapt your speech to evoke a more favorable response. You will be able to say the right things to strike a chord with your audience and persuade them. As a speaker, you'll discover a common ground for connecting with your audience for better results.

- Your chances of electing leaders, politicians and influencers with the right vision will increase when you learn to understand people's motives through their body language, personality, voice and words. Learn to identify traits that make for a powerful and positive influencer such as integrity, authority, generosity, empathy and more. You will be able to recognize people who truly care about others from those who display vested interests for grabbing power.

People are much like onions. They have multiple personality layers that have to be peeled off to glimpse into their real personality characteristics. Some layers of your personality are apparent, while others are inconspicuous. Sometimes, even we are unable to figure out who we really are because we seem like such a bundle of contradictions to ourselves.

A people analyzer or reader can quickly decipher an individual's personality through several attributes, including what he or she does in their spare time. For example, if you inquire what a person does in their spare time and they reveal they participate in community drives, volunteering activities or contribute to church initiatives, you know they are philanthropic, magnanimous or community conscious. Similarly, if a person says they love partying endlessly or watching television in their free time, they may be low on ambition or seek quick gratification. The point is, even something as seemingly trivial as what a person does in his or her spare time can reveal his or her personality.

Theories of Human Behavior

Classical Conditioning

Classical Conditioning is a popular psychological theory through which people learn by pairing behavior as stimuli and response to the stimuli. This principle is used for training animals too. Don't you reward your dog with a treat each time it fetches the ball? In the pet's mind, fetching is closely associated with treats or rewards, so it invariably learns that it has to fetch the ball if wants to be rewarded with a treat.

All through our life as human beings, classical conditioning helps shape our behavior. As babies, we come to associate crying with being fed and kept clean. Students learn that studying consistently and dedicatedly gets you good grades. Thus, classical conditioning influences our behavior and acts throughout our lives. We learn to respond to a specific stimuli in a particular manner. It is one of the main factors when it comes to determining an individual's behavior.

Human Behavior and Physiology

According to research, people have peculiar physical reactions to certain stimuli that are valuable when it comes to analyzing them. These principles are usually used in the area of criminal psychology to understand how criminals think and what drives them to commit crimes. With the help of biometric technology investigators attempt to identify if the suspect's thoughts are in sync with their actions.

This combination of psychological and physiological techniques is powerful for analyzing the underlying motives of human behavior. The human body undergoes specific physiological reactions when a person is misleading or lying. The reaction can be standalone clues or a combination of dilated pupils, increase in heart rate, greater palpitations, sweating and twitching toes. Physiology or non-verbal clues can help you analyze a person more accurately, though much like other people analyzing theories, it can never be fool proof.

Experiences and Human Behavior

While certain psychologists are of the opinion that our behavior is directly determined by genetics or heredity, others believe that it is a summation of all our experiences since birth. They are of the opinion that our immediate environment or the experiences we undergo in our immediate environment mold our behavior. For example, if a person experiences constant marginalization or prejudice on account of their class or race, they may grow up to despise wealth or seemingly superior races. They may empathize with the oppressed.

Similarly, if a person is constantly bullied, abused or victimized as a child, he or she may grow up to be a bully themselves. Much of their outlook, values, personality and attitude will be shaped by these early childhood experiences or violence and abuse.

Many psychologists believe that a person is almost always drawn to things they inherently believe they lack to make up for it. For instance, people who are not sure of themselves or don't have a high self-confidence or self-esteem may constantly seek approval from others. They may look for approval and validation all the time.

Have you ever observed people who keenly attempt read their personality through zodiac signs or astrology? Isn't this a sign of possessing low self-awareness or understanding? People often gravitate towards things they believe they haven't got much of. For example, someone who hasn't been given sufficient attention by their parents during early childhood or teen years may grow up to be a person who thrives on drama and attention-seeking tactics. They may become more dramatic and showy.

There are plenty of clues everywhere. As a people analyzer, you just need to keep an eye out for these subtle clues.

Subconscious Mind and Human Behavior

Our mind is divided into three layers – the conscious mind, subconscious mind and unconscious mind. While the conscious mind or state of consciousness is awareness of thoughts, actions, learnings and experiences, the subconscious and unconscious mind are realms of the mind that hold things we may not be aware of. Through the conscious mind, we have awareness of things we perceive and feel. We can process feelings, thoughts, concepts and ideas that are gathered from our immediate environment.

However, when it comes to the subconscious and unconscious mind, we have little or no awareness of the thoughts, ideas, concepts and information stored in it. Our conscious mind is only the tip of an iceberg. There are multiple hidden layers, which influence our personality and behavior that we are not aware of.

If you want to be a power-packed people analyzer, begin with yourself. Identify how much you know about yourself or how well you understand your own personality or behavior patterns. Attempt to understand what drives you into behaving in a specific manner. What are your underlying beliefs, fears, motivators, values and more?

Once you've uncovered your own personality and behavioral characteristics, attempt to understand close friends and family members. Lastly, move to strangers who you spot while waiting at a doctor's clinic or at the supermarket/airport or someone you've only just met at a party. Keep practicing to sharpen your people analyzing skills until you are able to read people quickly and effectively, like a pro!

Emotions and Human Behavior

Emotions are brief short conscious experiences that we experience as part of our mental activity. These feelings are not based in rational or logical thoughts. For example, even in the face of compelling proof that our friend is betraying us behind our back, we don't break ties with him or her and prefer to trust them.

As humans, we are prone to acting on impulses rather than logic, reasoning and evidence. People's behaviors are fundamentally shaped by emotions. Thus, understanding people's emotions gives us the power to comprehend and predict their actions, personality and behavioral patterns.

Chapter 2:

Body Language And Voice Basics Revealed

Do you know that people communicate much more through what they leave unspoken than what they actually say? Body language accounts for around 55 percent of the entire message during the process of communication. In a study conducted by Dr. Albert Mehrabian, it was revealed that only 7 percent of our message is communicated through words, while 38 percent and 55 percent is conveyed through non-verbal elements such as vocal factors and body language, respectively.

Generally, what people say is well-thought and constructed within their conscious mind. This makes it easier to manipulate or fake words for creating a desired impression. Our body language, on the other hand, is guided by more involuntary movements of the subconscious mind. It is near impossible to fake subconsciously driven actions that we aren't even aware of. When you train yourself to look for non-verbal clues, you understand an individual's thoughts, feelings, actions and more at a deeper, subconscious level. Try controlling the thoughts held within your subconscious mind and you'll know what I am saying.

People are perpetually sending subconscious signals and clues while interacting with us, a majority of which we miss because we are conditioned to focus on their words. Since primitive times, human communicated through the power of gestures, symbols, expressions and more in the absence of a coherent language. You have the power to influence and persuade people through the use of body language on a deeply subconscious level since it's so instinctive and reflex driven.

Here are some of the most powerful body language decoding secrets that will help you unlock hidden clues held in the subconscious mind, and read people more effectively.

Establish a Behavior Baseline

Create a baseline for understanding a person's behavior if you want to read him or her more effectively. This is especially true when you are meeting people for the first time, and want to guard against forming inaccurate conclusions about people's behavior. Establishing a baseline guards you against misreading people by making sweeping judgments about their personality, feelings and behavior.

Establishing a baseline is nothing but determining the baseline personality of individual based on which you can read the person more effectively rather than making generic readings based on body language. For instance, if a person is more active, fast-thinking and impatient by nature, they will want to get a lot of things done quickly.

They may fidget with their hands or objects, tap their feet or appear restless. If you don't establish a baseline for their behavior, you may mistake their mental energy for nervousness or disinterest, since the clues are almost similar. You would mistakenly believe the person is anxious when he/she is hyperactive.

Observe and tune in to an individual completely to understand their baseline. This helps you examine both verbal and non-verbal clues in a context. How does a person generally react in the given situation? What is their fundamental personality? How do they communicate with other people? What type of words do they generally use? Are they essentially confident or unsure by nature?

When you know how they normally behave, you'll be able to catch a mismatch in their baseline and unusual behavior, which will make the reading even more effective.

Look For a Cluster of Clues

One of the biggest mistakes people make while analyzing others through non-verbal clues is looking for isolated or standalone clues instead of a bunch of clues. Your chances of reading a person accurately increases when you look at several clues that point to a single direction rather than making sweeping conclusions based on isolated clues. For instance, let us say you've read in a book about body language that people who resort to deception or aren't speaking the truth don't look a person directly in the eye.

However, it can also be a sign of being low on confidence or possessing low self-esteem. Similarly, a person may not be looking at your while speaking because he/she is directly facing discomfort causing sunlight. You ignore all other signs that point to the fact that the person is speaking the truth or is confident (a firm handshake, relaxed posture etc.) and only choose to look at the single clue that he/she isn't maintaining eye contact to inaccurately conclude that the person is lying. Look for at least 3-4 clues to arrive at a conclusion. Don't make sporadic conclusions about how a person is thinking or feeling based on single clues.

For all you know a person may be moving in another direction, not because they aren't interested in what you are speaking about or looking to escape, but because their seat is uncomfortable.

If you think the person is disinterested, look for other clues such as their expressions, gestures, eyes and more to make more accurate conclusions. Include a wider number of non verbal clues to make the analysis more accurate.

Look at the Context, Setting and Culture

Some body language clues are universal – think smile or eye contact. These signals more or less mean the same across cultures. However some non-verbal communication signals may have different connotations across diverse cultures.

For example, being gregarious and expressive is seen as common in Italian culture. People speak loudly, gesticulate with their hands in an animated manner, and are generally more expressive.

However, someone from England may decipher this behavior as massively exaggerated or a sign of nervousness. Enthusiasm, delight and excitement are expressed in a more subtle manner in England. For the Italian, this retrained behavior may signify disinterest. While the thumbs-up is a gesture of good luck in the west, in certain Middle Eastern cultures it is viewed as rude. If you are doing business with people from across the world, understanding cultural differences before reading people is vital.

Similarly, consider a setting before making sweeping conclusions through non-verbal signs such as body language. For example, a person may display drastically different behavior when he's at work among co-workers, at the bar and during a job interview. The setting and atmosphere of a job interview may make an otherwise confident person nervous.

Head and Face

People are most likely experiencing a sense of discomfort when they raise or arch their eyebrows. The facial muscles also begin twitching when they are hiding something or lying. These are micro expressions that are hard to manipulate since they happen in split seconds and are subconscious involuntary actions.

Maintaining eye contact can be a sign of both honesty and intimidation/aggression. On the other hand, constantly shifting your gaze can be a non-verbal clue of deceit.

The adage that one's eyes are a window into their soul is true. People who don't look into your eyes while speaking may not be very trustworthy. Similarly, a shifting gaze can indicate nervousness.

The human eye movements are closely linked with brain regions that perform specific functions. Hence, when we think (depending on what or how we are thinking), our eyes move in a clear direction. For example, when a person is asked for details that he/she is retrieving from memory, their eyes will move in the upper left direction. Similarly, when someone is constructing information (or making up stories) instead of recalling it from memory, their eyes will shift to the upper right direction. The exact opposite is true for left-handed folks. When people try to recall information from memory, their eyes shift to the upper left, whereas when they try to create facts, the eyes move towards the upper left corner. A person who is making fictitious sounds or talking about a conversation that didn't happen, their eyes will move to the lateral left.

When there's an inner dilemma or conflict, a person's eyes will dart towards their left collarbone. This is an indication of an inner dialogue when a person is stuck between two choices. Increased eye movement from one side to another can signal deception. Again, look for a cluster of clues rather than simply analyzing people based on their eye movements.

Expanded pupils or increased blinking is a huge sign of attraction, desire and lust. A person may also display these clues when they are interested in what you are saying. If a person sizes you up by looking at you in an upward and downward direction, they are most likely considering your potential as a sexual mate or rival. Similarly, looking at a person from head to toe can also be a sign of intimidation or dominance.

When you are observing a person's face, learn to watch out for micro expressions that are a direct involuntary response based on feelings and thoughts. These reactions are so instinctive and happen in microseconds that they are impossible to fake. For example, when a person is lying, their mouth slants for a few microseconds and the eyes slightly roll.

How can you tell apart a genuine smile from a fake one? Pay close attention to the region around the person's eyes. If someone is genuinely happy, their smile invariably reaches their eye and causes the skin around the eyes to crinkle slightly. There are folds around the corner of the person's eyes if they are genuinely happy. Another clear sign of a genuine smile is a crow's feet formation just under the person's eyes. A smile is often used by people to hide their true feelings and emotions. It is near impossible to fake a smile (which is so involuntary and subconscious driven).

Even the direction of a person's chin can reveal a lot about their thoughts or personality. If their chin is jutting out, he/she may be a stubborn or obstinate about their stand.

Posture

When a person maintains an upright, well-aligned and relaxed posture, he/she is most likely in control of their thoughts and feelings and is confident/self-assured. Their shoulders don't slouch awkwardly, and the overall posture doesn't sag. On the other hand, a sagging posture can be a sign of low self-esteem or confidence. It can also mean placing yourself below others or subconsciously begging for sympathy.

When a person occupies too much space physically by sitting with their legs apart or broadening their shoulders, they are establishing their dominance or power by occupying more physical space.

Limbs

Pay close attention to people's limb movements when you are reading them. When a person is bored, disinterested, nervous or frustrated, they will fidget with an object or their fingers. Crossing arms is a big signal of being, closed, suspicious, uninspired or in disagreement with what you are saying. The person isn't receptive to what you are speaking about.

If you want to get the person to listen to what you are saying, open them up subconsciously first by changing the topic of conversation. Once they are in a more receptive state of mind, resume the topic. When a person crosses their arms or legs, they are less likely to absorb or be persuaded by what you say.

A person's handshake can reveal a great deal about what they think about themselves or their equation with the other person. For instance, a weak handshake is a sign of nervousness, low self-esteem, lack of confidence, submissiveness and uncertainty. Similarly, a crushing handshake can be an indication of dominance or aggressiveness. A firm handshake implies self-confidence and a sense of self-assuredness.

Observe the direction in which a person's feet are pointed. If they are pointed in your direction, it means the person is interested in what you are saying. On the other hand, if they are pointed away from you, the person is looking for an escape route. Feet pointing in your direction or leaning slightly towards you are huge non-verbal signals of attraction.

Legendary Hollywood talent scouting agent once famously uttered, "I don't have a contract with my clients. Just a handshake is enough." You can indeed tell volumes about a person simply through their handshake.

Tone

The tone of a person's voice can communicate a lot about the way a person is feeling or thinking. Look for any inconsistency in a person's tone. Does the tone and pitch vary throughout the conversation? This can be a signal that the person is experiencing a surge of emotions. Listen to the volume of a person's voice. Something may not be quite right if they are speaking in a softer or louder than usual manner. Observe if the person is using filler words rather than concise phrases or sentences. It can be a sign of nervousness or they may be buying time to make up stories.

A person's tone can convey emotions they try to conceal or are unable to express. They may say something flattering to you but their tone may be slightly sarcastic or bitter, which can be a giveaway to what they are truly feeling. It can indicate a more passive aggressive personality. The meaning of exactly the same words can change drastically when delivered using a different tone, volume and inflection.

Let's say the person ends their sentence on a higher note. Doesn't it sound more like a question than a definitive statement? Similarly, if the person finishes their sentence on a flat note, he/she is making a confident or assured statement. The former can indicate doubt, uncertainty or suspicion, while the latter can be an indication of authority.

Proxemics

Proxemics refers to the physical space maintained during communication between people, which reveals volumes about how they relate to each other. Haven't you experienced a feeling of discomfort when someone tried to invade your personal space or come closer than you appreciate? This person is most likely seeking acceptance from you or trying to make their way into your inner social circle.

On the other hand, if a person comes closer than intended during negotiations, he/she may be trying to intimidate you or subconscious coax you into accepting their conditions. The ideal distance to test a person's comfort level is to stand at a minimum distance of four feet from them. If the person appears open, they are welcoming into their personal space. Similarly, if they are rigid, don't jump into their personal space immediately. They may not be ready to include you into their personal zone.

Mirroring

Mirroring a person's body language is a wonderful way to establish a rapport with a person on a subconscious level. Closely observe a person's body language while they are interacting with you. How is their posture? What are the words they typically use? If they are leaning against the bar or table, follow suit. Similarly, if they sip on their drink, mirror their action. If you spot them resting their elbow on a table, mirror their action.

Mirroring a person's action gives the other person an impression that you are one among them. It works on a primordial level to create sense of affiliation, likeliness and belongingness even before spoken language was invented. Adapt your actions, posture, gesture and movements with the other person to give a feeling of "being one among them." If the person is following your actions, they are seeking acceptance or validation from you.

Chapter 3:

Reading People Through Personality Types

Personality analysis is a field that is constantly evolving and varied. There are varying schools of psychological thoughts and theories when it comes to studying an individual's personality. Some of the most popular personality analyzing schools include trait theory, social learning, biological/genetic personality influencer and more.

Personality refers to an individual's distinct characteristics connected to processing thoughts, feelings and emotions that eventually determine their behavior. It involves taking into consideration all the traits a person possess to understand them as an entity. Personality study also includes understanding the inherent differences existing between people where particular characteristics are concerned.

Here are some of the most common personality type classifications.

Type A, B, C and D

Type A personality people are at a bigger risk of contracting heart diseases since they are known to be more aggressive, competitive, ambitious, short-tempered, impatient, impulsive and hyper active. Type A personality theory was introduced in the 50's by Meyer Friedman and Ray Rosenman. These people are more stressed due to their constant need to accomplish a lot. They are always striving to be better than others, which invariably leads to greater anxiety and stress.

Type B people are more reflective, balanced, even-tempered, inventive and less competitive by personality. They experience less stress and anxiety, along with staying unaffected by competition or time constraints. A Type B personality person is moderately ambitious and lives more in the present. They have a steadier and more restrained disposition. Type B folks are social, modest, innovative, gentle mannered, relaxed and low on stress.

Later psychologists came up with other personality types, too, since they found the division into Type A and B more restrictive. They discovered that some people demonstrated a combination of both A and B Type traits. Thus, segregating people into only two distinct personality groups doesn't do justice to the classification. This lead to the creation of even more personality types!

Type C people have a more meticulous eye for detail. They are focused, curious and diplomatic. There tend to put other people's needs before theirs. They are seldom assertive, straightforward and opinionated. This leads to Type C folks developing pent up resentment, frustration, anxiety and depression. There is a propensity to take everything seriously, which makes them reliable and efficient workers.

This personality type also possess high analytic skills, logical thinking powers and intelligence. However, they need to develop the knack of learning to be less diplomatic and more assertive. Type C also needs to develop the ability to relax and let their hair down periodically.

Lastly, Type D personality people are known to hold a more pessimistic view of life. They are socially awkward and withdrawn, and do not enjoy being in the limelight. They are constantly worried about being rejected by people. Type D people are at a greater risk of suffering from mental illnesses such as depression owing to pessimism, pent up frustration and melancholy. Since the Type D personality doesn't share things easily with others, they suffer internally.

Psychoanalytic Theory

This theory is different from the regular personality classification theories in the sense that the analysis is based is not based on the responses of people about their personality, but a more in-depth study of people's personalities by glimpsing into their subconscious or unconscious mind. Since the analysis is based on a study on a person's subconscious mind, errors and instances of misleading the reader are eliminated.

In psychoanalysis, a person's words and actions are known to be disguised manifestations for their underlying subconscious emotions. The founding father of the psychoanalytic theory was Sigmund Freud, who was of the view that all human behavior is primarily driven by primitive instincts, passions, impulse and underlying emotions. He theorized that all human behavior is a direct consequence of the equation between our id, ego and superego.

Through the free association method that includes experiences, memories, dreams and more; Freud analyzed underlying emotions, thoughts and feelings that determine their attitude and behavior. Thus a majority of our behavior can be traced to our early childhood experiences that are still lingering in our subconscious mind, which we may or may not be aware of.

For example, if an individual demonstrates aggressive traits as an adult, it can be pinned down to the violence, harassment or bullying he/she experienced in their early childhood. Similarly, if a child comes from an environment where there were very high expectations from him/her and the parents were seldom happy with his/her accomplishments, he/she may constantly seek validation or acceptance from others. They may fear rejection.

Thus, a person's childhood experiences can help you determine their personality and read them even more effectively according to the psychoanalytic theory. The theory is still extensively used when it comes to helping people cope with depression, anger, stress, panic attacks, aggression, obsessive disorders and much more.

Carl Jung's Personality Classification Theory

Psychologist Carl Jung classified people on the basis on their sociability quotient into introverts and extroverts. Introverts are folks who are primarily inward driven, shy, withdrawn and reticent. They are more focused on their ideas and sensibilities than the external world around them. Introverts are known to be more logical, reflective and sensible by nature. They take time to crawl out of their box, and establish a rapport with others.

On the other hand, extroverts are outgoing, friendly, affable, social and gregarious people who live more in the present than worry about the future. They have a more positive and exuberant disposition, and are more than willing to accept challenges or changes.

After classifying people as introverts and extroverts, Jung received his share of brickbats from psychologists who believed that the classification was too restrictive to categorize every human being on the planet. Experts argued that a majority of people rarely demonstrated extreme introvert or extrovert tendencies. According to them only a majority of people possess extreme introvert or extrovert tendencies. Most people in fact possess a little bit of both, and their behavior differs according to the situation.

For instance, someone like me enjoys going out and spending time with people but I also value some time alone for reflection and contemplation every now and then. This neither makes me a hardcore extrovert or introvert but more of a combination of both – an ambivert.

Social Learning

This theory talks about how people pick up personality or behavioral traits from their immediate environment. It proposes that an individual's behavior is a result of their growing up conditions and environment. We pick up specific patterns and personality traits through our experiences. Social learning psychologists are of the view that all our behavior is learnt through our social experiences.

For example, if a person has been rewarded in a specific manner, he or she learns behavior through positive reinforcement and experiences. For example, someone throwing excessive tantrums may have learned through their experiences that drama gets them attention. Every time they want attention they know throwing tantrums will do the trick. At times, we don't have to experience something to learn behavior. Our mind is conditioned to use complex codes, information, actions, symbols and consequences. A majority of our observations and vicarious experiences drive our behavior, and help us imbibe specific personality traits.

Ernest Kretschmer's Classification

German psychologist Ernest Kretschmer's personality classification theory theorizes that a person's physical characteristics or personality traits determine the likelihood of a person suffering from mental ailments and their personality.

According to this personality classification, people are classified as Athletic, Pyknic, Dysplastic and Asthenic. Pyknic personality types are people who are round, stout and short. They demonstrate more extrovert traits such as gregariousness, friendliness and an outgoing disposition.

The Aesthetic personality types are people who have a slender and slim appearance. They have a fundamentally introvert personality. These are folks who have strong, athletic and robust bodies, and demonstrate more aggressive, enthusiastic and energetic characteristics.

Briggs Myers Personality Indicator

There are multiple personality tests that determine an individual's personality type based on a psychological analysis. One of the most widely used personality analysis tests is the Briggs Myers Personality Indicator. It is a comprehensive report that analyzes people's personalities based on how they perceive the world and make decisions.

The Briggs-Myers Personality Indictor was created by Isabel Briggs Myers and Katherine Briggs. It is based on Jung's theory but expounds on it through four primary psychological functions or processes such as sensation, thinking, feeling and intuition.

The MBTI emphasizes on one of the four primary functions dominating over other traits. The personality indicator operates on an assumption that everyone possesses a preference for the manner in which they experience the world around them. These inherent differences emphasize our values, motives, beliefs and interests, and thus determine an overall personality.

There are around 16 distinct personality types based on this psychological personality analysis theory. The Briggs-Myers test comprises several questions, where test respondents reveal their personality through their answers. This test is also widely used in areas such as determining a person's chances of success in a particular role and compatibility in interpersonal relationships.

In Myers Briggs personality theory, a personality type is determined when there is a clear preference for one style over another. Different letters connected with individual preferences helps determine the person's Myers Briggs personality type. For instance, if a person reveals a clear tendency for I, S, T and J, they have the ISTJ personality type.

Extraversion and introversion – The first letter of the Briggs-Myers personality type is related to the direction of one's energy. If a person is externally focused or focused on the external world, they show a preference for extraversion. On the contrary, if the energy is inward directed, the person shows a clear inclination for introversion.

Sensing and Intuition – The second letter is concerned with processing information. If an individual prefers dealing with information, has clarity, can describe what they see etc. then they show a distinct preference for sensing. Intuition, on the other hand, is related to intangible ideas and concepts. Intuition is represented by the letter "N."

Thinking and Feeling – The third letter reflects an individual's decision making personality. People who show an inclination for analytic, logical and detached thinking reveal a tendency for thinking over feeling. Similarly, people who show a preference for feeling are more driven by their values or what they believe in.

Judgment and Perception – The last letter of the Briggs-Myer Type Indicator shows a person's way of viewing the world. If an individual reveals a preference for going with the tide and he/she is more flexible in their approach towards responding to things as they arise, they are perception driven. However, if their thoughts are more planned, rigid and clearly structured, they show an inclination for judging (judgment).

1. **INTJ – Introverted, Intuitive, Thinking and Judging**

The INTJ personality type is primarily inventive, strategic, imaginative, resourceful and creative. They have a clear plan for everything. They are known to be original, analytical, independent thinking and resolute. They are good at planning, and executing plans into action. The INTJ personality type is perceptive when it comes to recognizing patterns and giving a clear logical reason for patterns.

They have a high sense of responsibility and commitment, and rarely quit something without completing it. They have high expectations not just from themselves but others too. The INTJ personality type makes for wonderful leaders, and also dedicated followers. These are generally the kind of people you want as original and independent thinking leaders.

2. ISTJ – Introverted, Sensing, Thinking, Judging

ISTJs are composed, quiet, reserved, serious and contemplative. They are primarily focused on living a secure, unruffled and peaceful life. These people are highly reliable, meticulous, disciplined, responsible and precision-oriented. They are logical, rational and practical. ISTJ folks possess a steady approach when it comes to fulfilling their objectives.

There is a deep respect for position, authority, establishment and a more conventional way of living. ISTJ people are concerned about maintaining order in their immediate physical space, work and life. If you are looking for administrators or managers for your business, these people may be a good fit.

3. ISFJ – Introverted, Sensing, Feeling, Judging

ISFJ people are quiet, kind, responsible conscientious. They are focused on fulfilling their responsibilities and obligations. There is a clear tendency for being practical, balanced and steady. They have an inherent need to place the feelings and needs of other people over theirs. ISFJ personality type people lean towards conventions and established norms. They don't believe in challenging customers, and are more concerned about leading a peaceful and secure life.

The ISFJ personality type is intuitively tuned in to the needs, emotions and feelings of other people. They have a deep service sense, and are suitable for vocations where they are needed to be of help to other people.

4. ESTJ – Extroverted, Sensing, Thinking and Judging

ESTJ people live in the moment, and have a high sense of appreciation for the present moment. They demonstrate a high sense of reverence for conventions, traditions and established customs, and they'll rarely go against it. ESTJ folks have a good idea about how things should be resolved speedily and effectively. This makes them a good fit for leadership positions. They are logical, rational, practical and innately realistic.

The ESTJ personality type excels at managing complex projects, and is focused on completing things with careful attention to details. They are reliable and dependable when it comes to accomplishing challenging tasks. The ESTJ personality type put in a lot into each task they undertake, which makes them efficient project managers or leaders. They place a lot of premium on law, justice, social order and security.

5. ISTP – Introverted, Sensing, Thinking and Perceiving

ISTP type people are inquisitive, curious and intelligent people who are always focused on knowing how everything works. They demonstrate a composed, peaceful and unruffled disposition. ISTP people also possess highly developed motor/mechanical skills and show an inclination for intense adventure. These people are more tolerant, flexible and adaptive by nature. They are excellent observers, people watchers and analyzers. ISTP folks are known to dive into the base of any situation before they come up with an actionable solution.

They will almost always emphasize on organizing facts, and establishing a precise cause and effect relationship. These are almost always the problem solvers, analyzers or solution providers that appear more logical and emotionally detached. Their solutions are more logically driven and less determined by emotions.

6. ISFP – Introverted, Sensing, Feeling, Perceiving

ISFP personality type people are shy, reflective, kind and sensitive. They avoid confrontation, arguments or heated conflict, and always focus on forming peaceful and harmonious relationships. ISFP people will avoid situations where there is scope for conflict. One distinct characteristic is the ISFP type's evolved sense of aesthetics. There is a higher tendency to be broadminded, adaptive and accommodating.

The ISFP folks aren't obstinate about their views, and posses a high sense of balance and appreciation for other people's views. They will agree to disagree with others in a graceful manner. ISFP type people are inventive, independent thinking and path-breaking original. They safeguard their space fiercely, and attempt to work within the given time frame with diligence. They live for the moment, and aren't too worked up about their future.

7. **ESTP – Extroverted, Sensing, Thinking, Perceiving**

ESTP personality type are outgoing folks who use a more rational, practical and logical approach while handling challenges. They focus on gaining fast results and solutions. ESTP people very efficient when it comes to analyzing people through multiple clues! They make for excellent psychologists, investigators and people analyzers. They are intuitive, and pick on both verbal and non-verbal clues effectively.

The ESTP personality type is action-oriented and practical, and prefers tangible actions over intangible ideas. They have a more problem solving, energetic, enthusiastic and proactive approach to life. They ESTP type people are more spontaneous, focused, random and attentive. Their ideal learning approach is hands on knowledge or learning by doing. They seek solutions by actively taking their problems head-on.

8. ESFP – Extroverted, Sensing, Feeling, Perceiving

ESTP type people are gregarious, flexible, amiable, loving and contemplative by nature. They seek new experiences, alternatives and possibilities. This personality type is also open for figuring out new ways to do things. They also like unique, unusual and off-beat stuff. These people are high on positivity and optimism.

They also make for exceptionally good team members, and love to combine their skills with other people to accomplish great results. These are folks who believe in living life queen or king size, while also developing solid relationships with others. The ESFP type is not very good when it comes to handling expectation, pressure and stress. They become pessimistic, negative and insecure.

9. ENTJ – Extroverted, Intuitive, Thinking and Judging

The ENTJ personality type is forthright, straightforward and outspoken, which makes them excellent leaders. According to them, the world is full of possibilities. Rather than perceiving problems as hurdles, they view them as challenges. ENTJ personality type people are ambitious, practical, career-minded and solution oriented.

They will consider problems from several angles before coming up with practical, effective and workable solutions. The ENTJ personality type is in its element when it comes to goal setting and fulfilling these goals. The ENTJ personality type are outspoken, clear decision makers and effortless leaders. For these people, the world is full of possibilities.

They are well-read, knowledgeable, abreast with what is happening in the world and more aggressive when it comes to expressing their ideas. While they may not be too intuitively connected to other people's feelings, ENTJs can be surprisingly emotional.

10.   INFP – Introverted, Intuitive, Feeling and Perceiving

The INFP personality type folks are balanced, composed, calm and contemplative. They are fiercely loyal and true to their value system. These people care deeply about others. They have a strong belief and value system, which guides them while making important decisions. The INFP people are loyal, adjusting, reliable, adaptable to change and relaxed. They easily empathize with other people, and reach to other people to make things easier for them.

11. INTP – Introvert, Intuitive, Thinking, Perceiving

INTP type people are independent thinking, creative, logical and analytic. They have a high sense of respect for knowledge and skills. By nature, they are reserved, reticent and withdrawn. They tend to exist in a world of their own and show little inclination for following others. The INTP personality type is fiercely independent and individualistic. They believe in creating their own route rather than following the one set by others.

12. ENFJ – Extroverted, Intuitive, Feeling and Judging

The ENFJ people have inherently well-developed people skills, and are known to be empathetic, kind, disciplined and affectionate. They are more externally focused and seldom enjoy being by themselves. The ENFJ people demonstrate an exceptional ability for spotting talent and skills in people. They also go out of the way to help people fulfill their real potential, thus making them wonderful leaders and managers.

One of the ENFJ personality type's best trait is their ability to accept praise and criticism with equal ease, while being faithful to people.

13. ESFJ – Extroverted, Sensing, Feeling and Judging

They ESFJ personality type are people who thrive when they are in the midst of other people. They are people persons, who enjoy interacting with other people, developing meaningful relationships with them, and getting to know them well. There is a huge need to be liked, admired and accepted by others. The ESFJ personality type desires that everything around them should be positive, balanced and harmonious for which they may go all out to support other people.

ESFJ people possess an inherent knack when it comes to making other people feel good about themselves. They will compliment and praise people lavishly in public, and ensure their strengths are highlighted. This personality type is popular because they have an inherent ability to make others feel special.

Their value or belief system is primarily guided by people around them, which makes them less rigid when it comes to their value system and beliefs. Also, they are more flexible when it comes to their different situations and persons. The ESFJ type enjoy being appreciated and are in their element when it comes to contributing to mankind's welfare. In any situation, they are concerned about the greater good.

14. ENTP – Extroverted, Intuitive, Thinking and Perceiving

The ENTP personality type is excited by ideas and concepts. They are able to analyze people and situations instinctively. They are fast decision makers and action takers. ENTP type people are also more alert, guarded, forthright and attentive. They are more fixated on possibilities or alternatives than plans.

They are excellent conversationalists who leave everyone bewitched with their words. ENTP don't like sticking to a routine, and are constantly seeking new experiences. They are experts at reading people, and have a deep sense of respect for learning. Again, they will consider multiple possibilities before zeroing down on a single solution.

15. ENFP – Extroverted, Intuitive, Feeling and Perceiving

The ENFP personality type people are fiercely independent, original and individualistic by nature. They believe in creating their own unique methods, habits, ideas, concepts and actions. This personality type doesn't fancy interacting with cookie clutter folks who follow the herd. They also despise being constrained in a box.

The ENFP personality type enjoys being around others and possess a strong sense of intuitive and sensitivity for others as well as themselves. They are more driven by emotions, and are known to be perceptive and contemplative. The ENFP personality type will think deeply about things from an emotional perspective before making a decision.

ENFP people are capable of accomplishing success in tasks that interest them. However, they also have a tendency to get easily bored doing things they aren't really good at. They don't fare too well when it comes to jobs that involve more meticulous, routine and detail-oriented tasks. They thrive in professions that allow them to express their creativity and come up with innovative ideas. Positions that are more confining and boxed will not appeal to them.

16. INFJ – Introverted, Intuitive, Feeling and Judging

The INFJ personality type are idealists, observers and visionaries who thrive on ideas and imagination. They have a unique and profound way of viewing the world. This personality type has the tendency to look at the world on a substantial and in-depth manner. They will seldom accept things as they are.

While others view the INFJ personality as weird or eccentric, they stick to their unusual views about life.

The INFJ people are compassionate, caring, gentle and complex individuals who are more inclined towards creative, independent and artistic endeavors. They reside in a world that filled esoteric possibilities. While this personality type places a high premium of order and organization, they can also be surprisingly spontaneous and intuitive.

They will be able understand ideas intuitively without pinpointing the reason. This makes the INFJ people less organized and systematic than other judging personality types.

Chapter 4:

Effectively Analyzing People Through Their Words

We don't use words mindlessly. There is a reason (often subconscious) behind our choice of words. The words we use are often guided by our subconscious feelings, emotions and thoughts. There is a clear underlying meaning behind phrases, words and other verbal expressions. Let us say for example, a person tells you that "Oh, so now you are dating another doctor." What does their choice of the word "another" indicate? It may imply that you just got out of a terrible relationship with a doctor, and fool hardily started dating another.

People use "yeah" and other similar terms when they want to communicate ambivalence. Similarly, they use "dude", "sis" or "bro" to express solidarity with people. It can be a sign of loyalty or friendship. There may also be a deep-seated need to be liked or accepted by the other person. People using these terms may seek to establish a sense of familiarity and belongingness with others. Begin by closely observing people's words and use it for peeking into the mind to unveil the thoughts and emotions behind their expressions.

Watch Out For Adjectives and Adverbs

The human brain is no short of a marvel. It is incredibly effective when it comes to thinking and vocalizing thoughts and/or ideas. When we think, our brains primarily use verbs and nouns. However, when we convert ideas or thoughts into language, we tend to elaborate on our thoughts by using adverbs and adjectives. These adverbs and adjectives that we use for describing basic nouns and verbs can reveal a lot about our inner feelings, thoughts and emotions. They can also offer a glimpse into our predominant values, and other ideas.

For example, let us consider a sentence such as "I ate". It comprises a pronoun and action verb. The words or expressions used to modify these sentences can offer plenty of information about a person. These are modifying words that give clues into an individual's value system or behavioral patterns. Through verbal expressions or clues, you can make a fairly reliable guess about an individual's state of mind or character. If you add "fast" to the above sentence, it indicates urgency.

They may eat fast because they are late for a meeting or are conscious about being punctual. It can reveal a more commitment-driven, responsible, dedicated and disciplined approach. They have a deep sense of respect for social norms, and may be focused on other's expectations. They may be your ideal employees since they are fast, punctual and committed. Of course, there can be plenty of other reasons why a person eats fast. However, descriptive words can offer you a good indication about people's thoughts, behavior and overall values.

Read Between the Lines

Not everything people say reveals a lot about them. Often, what they leave unsaid also says a lot about them. Even when someone offers you a compliment such as "You are looking cool today", it may not go down well with you. To you it may imply that you are looking cool only today and not every day. We subconsciously tune in to what is left unsaid.

Let us take another example to understand the hidden meaning behind words or what people leave unsaid. You take your friends out a newly opened restaurant in your neighborhood. It's a much talked about place and you just can't wait to try the stuff there. As soon as you enter, the waiter/server greets you warmly and directs your group to the table.

What follows is an elaborate seven course meal. Before serving you each of the scrumptious courses, the waiter introduces each course and tells you interesting details about the preparations. You have a great time wining and dining with friends. Once you finish the entire seven course meal, you request the waiter to bring your check.

The waiter brings over your check and asks you for your feedback about the food. You sum it up in a single line by stating, "The soup was good." The waiter doesn't react too positively and looks a tad disappointed. You wonder why! According to you, you just paid him/her a compliment. However, the things you left unsaid revealed a lot about your opinion or thoughts regarding the food.

The other person subconsciously latched on to what you left unsaid. It revealed that apart from the soup, nothing else was worth mentioning or everything other than the soup was average. While people communicate plenty through what they say, they leave a lot of things unsaid.

I Test

This is yet another verbal determinant of an individual's personality. If a person uses the term

"I" excessively, it indicates self-centeredness, selfishness or a large ego. However, the more "I" a person uses, the less powerful he/she feels. People who aren't sure about their power feel the desire to establish false sense of power through excessive usage of "I." Do a tiny exercise right now. Browse through the mails that are sent by people in a position of high authority. Now compare these mails will people who aren't in very authoritative positions, you'll clearly notice more usage of "I" in the latter.

For example, "Dear Jones, I was a student of your biology class last year. I have always enjoyed being a part of your classes. I've learned a lot through them. I received an email from you related to research collaboration. I would really appreciate working with you." Mr. Jones may reply with "That's amazing news. This week may be slightly busy for me owing to prior commitments. How about a meeting next Tuesday from 5 to 7? It will be wonderful to catch up."

Other than an indication of less power and higher self consciousness, it is also a clue of depression. A research published in Scientific Study of Literature revealed that illustrious poets who committed suicide frequently resorted to the usage of first-person pronouns while writing poetry.

Talking About Others

What people say about other people is often a reflection of their own personality. In a research conducted by Siminie Vazire and Peter Harms, it has been discovered that asking people to rate others on three negative and three positive aspects gave plenty of insights about their social personality, overall being, mental health and their view about others. It was found that a person's tendency to see others in a more positive light indicates their own positivity.

There is a powerful link between having an opinion about other people and possessing an energetic, courteous, optimistic, emotionally balanced and

84

kind personality. Talking positively about other people demonstrates how positively they view their own lives. On the other hand, people who use unflattering and negative words and phrases view themselves in an inferior light.

There is a greater correlation between using unflattering words used for describing other people and narcissism, low self-confidence, anti-social tendencies, frustration, overall dissatisfaction and more. People with a primarily negative personality type tend to view others in a more unflattering light. This can be a strong indication of mental issues, personality disorder or an unstable mind.

The Object Description Analysis

The manner in which a person describes an object is also enough to give you a fair idea about how the individual views the world, along with how he/she thinks and feels. The most commonly used cluster words will offer a clear basis for their behavior and personality. This linguistic personality determination technique is called meaning extraction.

Additional Words

The extra or additional words a person uses while conversing with you can reveal a lot about their thoughts, behavior and personality. For example, if someone says, "I won yet another award" in place of "I won an award", it reveals a need to tell people that they've won plenty of awards earlier. The individual may be struck with a terrible complex that makes them scream about their objection from rooftops.

Pick up this clue and learn that one of the best ways to develop a rapport with this person is to hail them for their accomplishments. Their words present an area of weakness that you can quickly cash on. Watch out for an incompatibility between the person's verbal and non-verbal clues. For example, an individual may state that they are delighted to meet you. However, if their body language is rigid, inflexible and uncomfortable, something may be wrong. A trained eye can easily figure out inconsistencies between a person's verbal and non-verbal signals.

You can fall back on their words and body language collectively to understand what the person is thinking or feeling.

"I Made Up My Mind" – Introverts and Extroverts

If an individual says he/she has made up their mind, they have most likely considered several options before making a clear decision. It implies that a person is prone to contemplating and reflecting upon their decision rather than making spur of the moment decisions. They have deliberated on their decision, and may be analytic or logical by nature.

There are lesser chances of them being rash, spontaneous and impulsive decision makers. The words are an indication of a person's introvertedness and extrovertedness. Taking decisions after giving it a thought is a sign of introvertedness.

However, guard against making instant, sporadic decisions about people based on the words they use. Simply using "decided" or "I made up my mind" isn't enough to make conclusions about an individual's personality. Identify a clear pattern and several verbal/non-verbal clues to read people more effectively. Watch out for clues that support your initial reading or point to contrary evidence.

Extroverts collect their energies from other people and their environment. They stimulation and decision making comes from using the trial and error technique over reflectively contemplating on their decision. Extroverts may speak more spontaneously without thinking, while introverts will carefully weight their words and its implications.

You can tailor your own communication pattern to suit the other person's once you get to know if they are an introvert or extrovert. Identifying whether a person is an introvert or extrovert helps you understand how someone makes decisions. For example, let us say you are selling insurance. You may have to determine what drives both the introvert and extrovert personality types to make a decision about buying insurance.

Introverts may be more reflective and mull over the options before making a decision, while extroverts are more prone to making quick decisions. If you notice a primarily introverted mindset, give people more time to think before making a decision. Pushing these folks to make a quick decision may backfire. They may get uncomfortable with the idea of being pushed into a decision.

If you are negotiating important businesses deals, you don't give introverts enough time to mull over the conditions, they may come up with a negative response. On the contrary, people who make fast decisions show sign of being extroverts. They can be pushed into making fast decisions. However, one of the most vital things to keep in mind is that people rarely demonstrate absolute introvert or extrovert tendencies. A majority of people are a combination of introvertedness and extrovertedness.

Chapter 5:

Personality And Birth Order

An individual's birth order can also reveal a lot of his or her personality. This isn't just restricted to pop psychology talk or mindless party chatter but based on a psychological analysis of how the person relates to their family members and how they are treated within the family based on their position or birth order. A person's family dynamics plays a considerable role in shaping their personality. The role they fulfilled as children or during their adolescent years influences their behavior as adults. Our status quo as children establishes the foundation for our actions as adults. Notice how several times children born in the same family or raised in the same environment have dramatically diverse personalities.

Of course, there are other factors that in combination with a person's birth order can determine their personality type. These factors such as the family's overall socio-economic status, education, number of children in the family, parent's professional achievements and more also impacts an individual's personality.

It was Alfred Adler who first came up with the theory of studying an individual's personality through their birth rank. He used it a method for reading the behavior, personality and actions of his clients. However, it was Frank Sulloway who elaborated on the theory in his publication *Born to Rebel*. Sulloway's book identified five primary traits like extraversion, agreeableness, neuroticism, consciousness and openness.

The psychologist mentioned that an individual's birth order impacts their personality even more than their environment. This means that the chances of two first-borns having the same personality type is higher than two children belonging to one family.

Here are some ways to read a person through their birth order.

First-borns

First born children are known to be responsible and ambitious leaders, who pave the way for others. They are original, creative and independent thinking by nature. Since they get more undivided attention and time with their parents, they have a clear edge over their siblings. Again, they are more proactive and take the lead when it comes to caring for the siblings, which makes them more disciplined, inspiring, responsible and accountable as adults. They are protective towards those weaker than them, and often lead others.

If parents place a lot of expectations on the first in a household, the person may grow up feeling inadequate. This may not just lead to low self esteem but also a weak personality that is marked by a constant need for validation, acceptance and approval. The person may end up feeling that they can never be good enough for anything.

First born individuals are more goal-oriented and ambitious. They give plenty of importance to accomplishments and success. They thrive in or perform well in positions of authority, responsibility and maintaining discipline. There is an inherent tendency to be a control freak, while also being autocratic, dictatorial and bossy.

Owing to the fact that come first in the sibling hierarchy, these people are physically stronger than other children in the household, which gives them a marked dominant personality. They may have a high sense of entitlement.

First-borns are often high on determination, rule enforcement and attention to details.

Middle-borns

Since they are caught between two siblings, middle-borns develop a more complicated personality. They are neither given the rights and responsibilities of the older sibling nor the special privileges of the youngest sibling. This makes them look outside the home for friendships and connections.

Middle-borns often have very big social circles and are known to be excellent diplomats and negotiators. They are social creatures who function with a profound sense of peace and fairness. Middle-borns are fiercely loyal to their loves ones and seldom betray people's trust. Typical personality traits of middle born children are flexibility, generosity and adaptability. They are known for their diplomatic nature, and can play peacemakers in any situation.

Middle born children are primarily understanding, co-operative and adjusting. They also turn out to be competitive adults. Middle-borns have a close-knit social circle who award them the affection they haven't received within their family. Middle-borns are late raisers, and discover their calling after plenty of experimentation, contemplation and deliberation. They are at the center of authoritative careers that allow them to utilize their power-packed negotiation skills.

Middle-borns are generally social and operate with a deep sense of justice and fairness. Their typical personality characteristics include generosity, diplomacy, flexibility and adaptability. They are good at teamwork, and relate well with people belonging to multiple personality types since they have learnt to deal with older and younger siblings. Middle-borns display a more affable nature, and they know how to wriggle themselves out of confrontations and conflicts. They are known to be resourceful and quickly master multiple skills.

Last Born

By the time the youngest child of the family is born, parents are well-versed in their parenting skills and more economically settled. This makes them less paranoid and more secure. They aren't excessively monitored, which makes them more independent and freedom. Last born are excellent decision makers, and operate with a high sense of entitlement.

The last born is known to be charming and risk taking. They are independent thinking, original and adventurous. There is a greater tendency to rewrite the rules rather than following set norms.

Parents are less careful when it comes to their last born because they've already experienced being a parent, which helps them give more leeway and flexibility to the youngest child. Also, there are higher chances of pampering and indulging the child owing to a better financial status. Since parents are more relaxed and lenient with last-borns, they don't turn out to be conformists. They are used to plenty of attention, and they don't worship authority.

Rather than walking on set paths, they will create their own path. Since they've learnt to compete with their siblings for their parent's time and attention, they are good are handling competition and aren't easily bothered by feelings of envy and insecurity.

Since they are more creative and independent thinking, they thrive in careers such as stand up comedians, painters, dancers and authors. Typical personality characteristics include empathy, obstinacy, extroversion, manipulativeness, penchant for drama and more. These are your salespeople, since they are glib and can talk themselves of almost any situation.

Sole Child

The only child doesn't have to complete with anyone for their parents' time and attention, which makes them self-centered. There is a tendency to think that everything revolves around them. They tend to spend a lot of time alone, which turns them into more original, resourceful, inventive and creative people. Sole or only children find new and innovative ways to keep themselves busy. By nature, they are more confident, self-assured, meticulous, expressive and firm. They express their opinions more assertively and confidently.

Since they do not have to deal with sibling rivalry of any kind, they are always used to having things their way. They become edgy and unsettled when they have to complete with others or things don't go their way. Sole-borns find it tough to share the limelight with others. They almost always want to be the center of attention since they've never had to complete with any for attention at home through their childhood and adolescent years. Only-borns are constantly seeking attention, respect and attention. In the absence of siblings as role models, their only role models are elders of the house. Since grown-ups become their role models, they grow up to be perfectionists.

There are multiple factors that impact a person's behavioral characteristics and personality. To make a more accurate reading an individual's personality through birth order, there are some effective tips offers by psychologists. They recommend analyzing a person's siblings while reading their personality since no two children in the same household ever share the same role. If one assumes the role of a caretaker, the other will invariably be the care recipient.

Other factor that are taken into consideration while analyzing an individual's personality through birth order is genetics, gender, social status and other factors (apart from their birth order). These factors together will help you make more accurate readings about an individual's personality than simply relying on birth order.

Conclusion

I genuinely hope this book has offered you multiple invaluable insights about reading people's personality through well-researched strategies, tried and tested techniques and a bunch of practical tips. These tips can be applied in just about any situation from professional to interpersonal relationships to your social life.

Whether you want to figure out the personality of a prospective buyer during a negotiation or the personality traits of the new date you have your eyes on, this book is a valuable resource for helping you read others effectively. If there's a single largest skill that translates into success in modern times, it is the knack of reading people.

When you know how a person thinks or feels, you can mould your message according to his or her personality for accomplishing an optimally beneficial outcome.

The next step is to use this book and apply it in your everyday life in tiny, gradual ways to start with.

Begin by observing people at the airport, supermarket or doctor's clinic when you have free time. You'll become more interested in the art of analyzing people, and find yourself doing it at every given opportunity.

Finally, if you enjoyed reading the book, please take the time to share your views by posting a review of Amazon. It'd be highly appreciated!

How To Analyze People 2

Learn Rapid Deduction Techniques To
Think And Analyze People Like Sherlock
Holmes

Patrick Lightman

Introduction

Imagine possessing the ability to decipher within a couple of meetings if a prospective date has it in him or her to be a supportive, compatible and inspiring long-term partner. Imagine telling through a potential client's verbal and nonverbal clues if he or she will negotiate on your terms. Imagine being able to decode though a prospective buy's clues if he or she is likely to buy from you. Is a business associate satisfied with your terms and conditions to go ahead with a deal? Is the salesperson trying to mislead you into buying or are they speaking the truth? Can you read people's reactions to steer the communication in a favorable direction?

This is the power of being able to analyze people's reactions. You can predetermine the outcomes of different communication styles and adapt the one that suits the other person the most to accomplish a beneficial outcome.

Plenty of conflicts we experience in our daily lives are entrenched in our inability to read or analyze other people accurate. We fail to understand how they are thinking and feeling, which creates misunderstandings. Then again, our inherent insecurities are all rooted in what people think about us. Will my partner cherish my existence in their life? Does he or she value me? Does my manager appreciate my skills? These are the most inherent fears that we operate with. Once we learn to read people, these insecurities and uncertainties don't bog us down.

Knowing how to speed read people accurately is nothing short of a superpower or secret magic weapon. Imagine possessing the super power to quickly read a person like a book. You will be eliminating tiresome guesswork from relationships and focus on communicating with a person that is most suitable for his or her thoughts, feelings and personality.

When we learn to become more telepathic and master the knack of reading other people, we can use our cards in a manner that is beneficial for us. You don't have to develop the knack of being an FBI style investigator to analyze people or understand how they think and feel. All you need to do is watch out for verbal and non-verbal clues that the person is constantly giving out to know what they are thinking.

A person is consciously and subconsciously giving out plenty of clues about not just what they are currently thinking and feeling but also their overall personality, ideologies, values, attitude, preferences and much more. You only have to be perceptive enough to tune in these clues at a subconscious level.

I recently read a piece about how what the content you like on Facebook can help determine everything from your sexual preferences to gender to relationship status. Imagine, your social media likes determining your subconscious persona. There are plenty of clues of everywhere; you just need to watch out for them.

Even when we don't realize, people are constantly giving away signals about how they are thinking and feeling. When you know exactly what to look for, your intuition, perceptiveness and subconscious communication increases multi-fold. At times, you don't understand people because you aren't actively tuning in to these signals. People are nothing short of an enigma and learning to watch out for the right clues allows you to put together prices of a challenging puzzle.

Our knack for analyzing people influences the manner through which we interact with them. When you understand how a person processes information and emotions, the message can be delivered in a manner that is most beneficial for everyone involved.

According to research conducted by MIT, the other person's body language is an accurate giveaway about the outcomes of the negotiation 80 percent of the time. This implies that the person is offering clues about their inner feelings and thoughts involuntarily almost all the while.

An individual's overall personality is a sum total of several attributes, including beliefs, learnt behavior, childhood experiences, gender roles, birth order, peer influence, genetics, environment and others. All these factors are noticeable in the way people speak and conduct themselves.

While a layperson may view people itching their nose as a seemingly harmless or reflex gesture, a people analyzer will always seek deeper meaning in the action.

For instance, if a person has been confronted with facts where their lies have been called out and they start scratching their nose, he or she may most likely be lying. These gestures happen at such a subconscious level that the person isn't even aware that they are sending out these signals or doing these gestures, which makes these verbal and non-clues almost impossible to fake. These gestures are directed by the subconscious mind and are more reflex actions than awareness driven behavior.

Research has it that a person retains around 10 percent of the information imparted verbally, and 20 percent of visually communicated information. However, we remember around 80 percent of the information that is conveyed using a combination of both verbal and non-verbal communication methods. This also means that if you combine both verbal and non-verbal communication clues, your chances of being an effective and persuasive communicator will increase.

Body language along with other non-verbal clues is important when it comes to analyzing people. When a person's non-verbal clues match their verbal clues, it is a sign of confidence, authenticity, trustworthiness and clarity. On the contrary, if there is a clear mismatch between a person's verbal and nonverbal clues, it can indicate mistrust, deceit and lies. The person may not be telling the truth or may be trying to hide something. Even lack of non-verbal clues can be an indication that a person is not telling the truth or trying to contrive /manipulate his actions to conceal his or her true feelings and thoughts.

Chapter 1:

Analyzing People Through Their Handwriting

Every person's handwriting is known to be as unique as their personality. You can make an in-depth analysis about everything from their behavior to personality to thought process. Graphology is the science of studying an individual's personality through how they write. Handwriting goes beyond putting a few characters on paper. It is about glimpsing into an individual's mind to decipher what they are thinking and how they are feeling based on their handwriting.

Here are some little-known secrets about speed reading a person through their handwriting.

Analyzing Individual Letters of the Alphabet

The manner in which a person writes his or her letters offers a huge bank of information about their personality, subconscious thoughts and behavioral characteristics. There are several ways of writing a single letter, and every person has their own distinct way of constructing it.

For example, putting a dot on the lower case "I" is an indication of an independent-spirited personality, originality and creative thinking. These folks are organized, meticulous and focused on details. If the dot is represented by an entire circle, there are pretty good chances of the person being more childlike and thinking outside the box. The manner in which a person constructs their upper case "I" reveals a lot about how they perceive themselves. Does their "I" feature the same size as the other letters or is it bigger/smaller compared to other letters?

A person who constructs a large "I" is often egoistic, self-centered, over confident and even slightly cocky. If the "I" is the size of other letters or even smaller than other letters, the person is more self-assured, positive and happy by disposition.

Similarly, how people write their lower case "t" offers important clues into their personality. If the "t" is crossed with a long line, it can be an indication of determination, energy, passion, zest and enthusiasm. On the other hand, a brief line across the "t" reveals lack of empathy, low interest, and determination. The person doesn't have very strong views about anything and is generally apathetic. If a person crosses their "t" really high, they possess an increased sense of self-worth and generally have ambitious objectives.

Similarly, people who cross their "t" low may suffer from low self-esteem, low confidence and lack of ambition. A person who narrows the loop in lower case "e" is likelier to be uncertain, suspicious and doubtful of people. There is an amount of skepticism involved that prevents them from being trustful of people. These people tend to have a guarded, stoic, withdrawn and reticent personality.

A wider loop demonstrates a more inclusive and accepting personality. They are open to different experiences, ideas and perspectives.

Next, if an individual writes their "o" to form a wide circle, they are most likely people who very articulate, expressive, and won't hesitate to share secrets with everyone. Their life is like an open book. On the contrary, a closed "o" reveals that the person has a more private personality and is reticent by nature.

Cursive Letters

Cursive writing gives us clues about people that we may otherwise miss through regular writing. It may offer us more comprehensive and in-depth analysis of an individual's personality.

How does a person construct their lower case cursive "I?" If it has a narrow loop, the person is mostly feeling stressed, nervous and anxiety. Again, a wider loop can be a sign that the individual doesn't believe in going by the rule book. There is a tendency to rewrite the rules. They are laidback, low on ambition and easy going.

Again, consider the way a person writes cursive "y" to gain more information about their personality. The length and breadth of letter "y" can be extremely telling. A thinner and slimmer "y" can be an indication of a person who is more selective about their friend circle. On the other hand, a thicker "y" reveals a tendency to get along with different kinds of people. These are social beings who like surrounding themselves with plenty of friends.

A long "y" is an indication for travel, adventure, thrills and adventures. On the other hand, a brief cursive "y" reflects a need to seek comfort in the familiar. They are most comfortable in their homes and other known territories. A more rounded "s" is a signal of wanting to keep their near and dear ones happy. They'll always want their loved ones to be positive and cheerful.

They will seldom get into confrontations and strive to maintain a more balanced personality. A more tapering "s" indicates a hard-working, curious and hard-working personality. They are driven by ideas and concepts. Notice how cursive "s" broadens at the lower tip. This can be a strong indication of the person being dissatisfied with their job, interpersonal relationships or life in general. They may not pursue their heart true desires.

Letter Size

This is a primary observation that is used for analyzing a person through their handwriting. Big letters reveal that the person is outgoing, affable, gregarious and extrovert. They are more social by nature and operate with a mistaken sense of pride. There is a tendency to pretend to be something they aren't. On the contrary, tiny letters can indicate a timid, reticent, introvert and shy personality. It can indicate deep concentration and diligence.

Midsized letters mean that an individual is flexible, adjusting, adaptable and self-assured.

Gap Between Text

People who leave a little gap in between letters and words demonstrate a fear of leading a solitary life. These people always like to be surrounded by other folks, and often fail to respect the privacy and personal space of other people. People who space out their words/letters are original thinkers and fiercely independent. For them, they place a high premium on freedom and independence. There is little tendency for being overwhelmed by other people's ideas, opinions and values.

Letter Shape

Look at the shape of an individual's letters while decoding their personality. If the writing is more rounded and in a looped manner, the person tends to be high on inventiveness and imagination!

Pointed letters demonstrate that a person is more aggressive and intelligent. The person is analytical, rational and a profound thinker. Similarly, if the letters of an alphabet are woven together, the individual is methodical, systematic and orderly. They will rarely work or live in chaos.

Page Margins

If you thought it's only about writing, think again. Even the amount of space people leave near the edge of the margin determines their personality. Someone who leaves a big gap on the right side of the margin is known to be nervous and apprehensive about the future. People who write all over the page are known to have a mind full of ideas, concepts and thoughts. They are itching to do several things at once, and ae constantly buzzing with ideas.

Slant Writing

Some people show a marked tendency for writing with a clear right or left slant, while other people write impeccably straight letters. When a person's letters slant towards the right, he or she may be affable, easy going, good natured and generally positive. These people are flexible, open to change and always keen on building new social connections.

Similarly, people who write slanting letters that lean towards the left are mostly introverts who enjoy their time alone. They aren't very comfortable being in the spotlight and are happy to let others hog the limelight. A straight handwriting indicates rational, level headed and balanced thinking. The person is more even-tempered, grounded and ambivalent.

There is a tiny pointer here to avoid reading people accurately. For left-handed people, the analysis is the opposite. When left handed people have their letters slanting to the right, they are shy, introverted and reserved. However, if their letters slant to the left, they may be outgoing, gregarious and social extroverts.

Writing Pressure

The intensity with which an individual writes is also an indicator of their personality. If the handwriting is too intense and full of pressure (there is indentation), the individual may be fiery, aggressive, obstinate and volatile. They aren't very open to other people's ideas, beliefs and opinions. There is a tendency to be rigid about their views.

On the contrary, if a person writes with little pressure or intensity, they are likely to be empathetic, sensitive and considerate towards other people's needs. These people tend to be kind, enthusiastic, passionate, lively and intense.

Signature

A person's signature reveals plenty about an individual's personality. If it isn't comprehensible, it is a sign that he or she doesn't share too many details about themselves. They fiercely guard their private space and are reticent by nature. On the contrary, a more conspicuous and legible signature is an indication of a self-assured, flexible, transparent, assured, confident and satisfied personality. They are generally content with what they've accomplished and display a more positive outlook towards life.

Some people scrawl their signature quickly, which can be an indication of them being impatient, restless, perpetually in a hurry and desiring to do multiple things at one time. A carefully written and neatly organized signature is an indication of the person being diligent, well-organized and precision-oriented.

Signatures that finish in an upward stroke demonstrate a more confident, fun loving, ambitious and goal-oriented personality. These people thrive on challenges, aren't afraid of chasing these dreams. Similarly, signatures that finish with a downward stroke are an indication of a personality that is marked by low self-esteem, lack of self-confidence, low ambition and a more inhibited personality. These folks are likelier to be bogged down by challenges and may not be too goal oriented.

Stand Out Writing

If a particular piece of writing stands out from the other text, look at it carefully to understand an individual's personality.

For example, if the text is generally written in a more spread out and huge writing, with only some parts of the text stuck together, the person may most likely to be an uncertain, dishonest or mistrustful individual, who is trying to conceal some important information.

Concluding

Though studying an individual's handwriting can offer you accurate insights about his or her personality, it isn't completely fool proof. There are several other factors that are to be taken into consideration to analyze a person accurately. It has its own shortcomings and flaws. At times, people may write in a hurried manner, which can impact their writing. Similarly, the way people construct their resume or application letter may dramatically vary from the manner in which they may write a to-do list or love letter.

If you want an accurate reading of someone's personality, consider different personality analysis methods like reading verbal and non-verbal communication techniques. Various techniques may offer you a highly in-depth, insightful, precise and comprehensive method of understanding a person's inherent personality.

Chapter 2:

Tips For Uncovering Insights About Other People's Values

Mind reading isn't about drinking some magic potion and developing telepathic powers overnight. It is a science that is carefully nurtured and mastered by people to attain success in their daily life. Reading or analyzing people is a valuable skill that can come handy in any situation from approaching your manager for a raise to understanding a customer's needs to impressing a prospective date.

Here are some proven tips for deciphering people's values, wishes and desires through their thoughts, behavior and actions.

Watch For Hot Buttons

What are the emotional stimulants of a person you are studying? What is their comfort zone? Identifying people's emotional triggers is a great way of gaining insight into their beliefs, value system and wishes.

A handy tip for learning more about a person's ideologies and values is to pose open ended questions to them. Rather than asking close-ended yes/no questions, pose queries that urge them to offer more in-depth responses. This can provide a glimpse into an individual's values.

Watch Out For Generational Differences

Though this is not a 100 percent fool proof method for analyzing a person's values, it can be an effective baseline for reading their personality through the manner in which they view the world. Generational differences may be more fascinating and insightful than people believe. While millennials focus on establishing more non-personal communication channels through social media or messenger.

On the other hand, bloomers may prefer face to face interactions where they can establish more meaningful and personal connections with others. They seek to set-up relationships where verbal and non-verbal signals are effective to make the most of their communication. Identifying an individual's generation can help to read them or try to establish a favorable rapport with them.

For example, if you want to close the deal with a youngish CEO you know there are lower chances of them wanting to complete the formalities face to face. They may be people who are comfortable with technology and sending emails back and forth. Their value system or way of working may be more determined by technology than by the old-fashioned route of taking potential clients and business associates on elaborate lunches and dinners. Knowing a person's generation can help you gain insights into another person's values, beliefs and principles.

Handling Power and Authority

The manner in which a person handles power reveals a lot about their values, beliefs and character. What is the individual's overall attitude towards people who they perceive to be lower in status? How do they treat servers, waiters and other people who can't do much for them or who we perceive to be beneath us in the status quo?

Listen to them talk to a customer service personnel. How do they air their grievances? What is the person's overall outlook towards animals and children? The way people treat other people who can't return their favors says a lot about their values. Are they generally rude to individuals who aren't as powerful as them? Do they indulge in more magnanimous or selfless acts? This reveals an individual's real colors.

Look at the Person's Contact List

It isn't a secret that a man is known for the company he keeps. One of the best ways for gaining insights into a person's value system and needs is through their friend circle. Are they with the same set of people since the last few years? Are they the leaders or followers within their social circle? Do they influence other people or are they influenced by the decisions and tastes of others? What are the types of people they dislike and like?

When you want to know more about someone's values, attitude, beliefs and principles, ask them about the type of people they avoid. This is a brilliant way to know their ideologies. They will always avoid people whose values clash with theirs. For example, when people I pose this question to tell me that they avoid people who are high-handed or deceitful, it is evident that they are more drawn towards honest and down to earth folks. Similarly, a person who says he/she don't like to mingle with people who are always partying may be more focused, goal-oriented and hard working. They are hard-working and want to achieve a lot in life.

If you notice carefully, you will identify a clear pattern in everyone they avoid. These traits reveal their own set of values. For example, sometimes you will notice that you just won't like certain people or you may subconscious avoid them. On closer scrutiny, you'll realize that they may all be ineffective listeners who do not show consideration for other people's thoughts, opinions, beliefs and feelings.

They may be more focused on being heard and putting their point across than listening to others. All this will help you realize that people who dislike or avoid such people may boast of a more empathetic personality that places a high premium on tuning in to other people's emotions.

Language

A person's beliefs, values, desires and principles are to a large extent revealed by their words. According to psychologists, we tend to emphasize on adjectives than pronouns while speaking, which offers subconscious indications of our persona. A high number of personal pronouns demonstrate an egocentric, selfish and self-centered personality. It can also be an indication of increased self-awareness, honesty, integrity.

There are other things that determine an individual's personality. For example, if a person is using big words or fancy terms to expresses their point of view, he or she may possess a desire to be constantly accepted or validates by others. There is a strong tendency to fit in or impress others. The individual may have faced rejection during their childhood, which led them to develop low self-confidence, low self-esteem and feeling of never being good enough.

On the other hand, people who use simpler words and phrases to express themselves are logical, self-assured and rational people who are confident in their abilities. They don't seek acceptance or validation from others and are fairly firm in their decision making. People who use words such as "but", "except" and "without" are mostly honest and truthful people who won't hesitate to share details.

Notice how people who are mostly happy, positive and content do not use "I" often. Similarly, usage of "he", "they" "she" etc. are more focused on others. They place the other person first in a relationship, while their own needs are put on the backburner. Even the kind of humor and jokes a person shares can tell a lot about their values, character, personality and attitude.

Don't we all love celebrities to engage in self-depreciating humor? Or for that matter anyone who cracks jokes about themselves! It is a sign of high confidence, self-assuredness and self-esteem. These people are confident and secure enough to poke fun at themselves. They don't think or care much about the opinion other people hold of them, which makes them take potshots at themselves freely.

On the other hand, people who are quickly offended by jokes directed towards them may not have a very high self-esteem or may be suffering from an inferiority complex. A deep seated feeling of insecurity or an inferiority complex makes them easily offended by jokes directed towards them. Thus a person's approach to humor along with the language they use can offer plenty of insights into their value system.

Reaction to Criticism

The manner in which a person responds to criticism reveals plenty about their values. What is a person's reaction to facing criticism? Do they get defensive, angry and foul mouthed? Do they fly into a quick fit of rage? Do they accept their shortcomings with grace? People who handle criticism with graceful are more confident, self-assured, frank and forth coming! They aren't egoistic by nature and consciously work on their limitations.

On the contrary, people who don't take criticism too well may most likely be suffering from an inferiority complex, low self-esteem and inflated ego issues. They may need constant validation and appreciation. In their eyes, they can seldom be wrong. These folks may suffer from a high sense of self-entitlement or a misplaced sense of self-importance. They tend to be egoistic, self-centered and selfish by nature, which means you'll have to employ a lot of tact and diplomacy while dealing with these people.

How Does a Person Spend Their Money and Time?

Time and money are some of the most important resources of a person's life, and the manner in which he or she utilizes these precious resources says a lot about their values. Do people spend a lot of time and money on building a solid long-term future for themselves of their loved ones? Do they focus on acquisition of knowledge, learning, classes, skills and education?

Do they utilize their free time for upgrading their skills or waste it on frivolous pursuits? What are their pursuits, interests and hobbies? Don't scan people's expenses with a magnifying glass now. All you need to do is observe how people use their valuable

Gut Feeling

We can master all the people analyzing methods of the world and still rely on our gut feeling when it comes to reading people. If you have a specifically terrible feeling about someone and can't peg it to a logical thought, it may be an instinctive or gut feeling.

If you think your intuition or gut feeling isn't rooted in a scientific process, think again. What is termed a scientific process is closely connected to the limbic brain. It is a reaction to subconscious clues that the conscious mind has missed. If you develop a feeling that something or someone isn't right, your gut feeling may be bang on.

A Person's Reaction to No

How a person reacts to someone who refuses their request says a lot about them. Are they respectful and graceful in the face of rejection? Do they accept it graciously? Do they respond in a more violent, aggressive and volatile manner? Do they respect people's wishes and boundaries? Does the person manipulate people into turning their no into a yes? How a person reacts to refusals can speak volumes about their values and character.

Chapter 3:

Reading People Through Their Immediate Environment

An individual's immediate environment can speak a lot about their personality, thought process, behavioral traits and values. Of course, this isn't a pop psychology quiz that pops on your social media timeline every now and then about your hairstyling preferences and nail paint colors determining your personality. These are solid, proven and scientific methods for making an educated guess about people through their immediate environment or the manner in which they live. There are clear psychological concepts and principles based on which you can tell a lot about a person through their environment. Here are some fabulous tips for analyzing a person through their surroundings.

The Closet

The mess within your physical environment is indicative of the chaos in the mind. This isn't about judging people through their environment; it is about analyzing people through their thought driven actions. It is reading a person through their thoughts, which eventually leads to the creation of the immediate environment.

A well-organized, efficient and systematic work station or desk is indicative of clear thoughts, clarity of decisions, good time management skills, and a need to get things done. The person is more goal driven and is driven by a desire to take up challenging tasks.

On the contrary, a messy, unclean and disorganized desk can be an indication of a chaotic mind that is filled with nervous and anxious thoughts. These people may suffer from low self-esteem, low self-confidence and other issues. It can also been observed that excessive cleanliness can be a sign of mental disorders like obsessive compulsive disorder and reveal a more nervous or anxious mind that is filled with uncertainties and a low self-esteem. There is an obsessive need to keep spaces clean and organized, which reveals a sense of inadequacy and disorderliness in the mind. The person may be trying to compensate for something they believe they lack by keeping their surroundings extra clean.

What is the first thing you think when you see a disorderly work or home space? Again, this isn't about being judgmental but reading or analyzing people through their immediate environment and setting. A cluttered space is often an indication of a cluttered mind. It can also mean that the person is a multi-tasker, who is keen on getting several things at a time. People who are busy or engaged in multiple activities seldom have the time or energy to organize their work space. As a result, it is left unattended or in a complete disarray. At times, a disorganized space can signal a plain lazy personality that reveals lack goals and clarity in life.

Again, you'd need to know more y digging a little deep rather than making sweeping judgments based on the space alone. It has been noticed that folks with a gregarious and social personality thrive in chaos around them. Peek into their drawers, and they are most likely kept in a disorganized and predictably messy manner. They aren't inward driven or believe in giving time to reflection, thoughts and organizing their space.

Introverts, on the other hand, are more reflective and contemplative y nature. Since they are inward directed, a lot of their time is spent in diligently organizing, arranging, managing and prioritizing their things. These things give them more clarity of thought and ideas upon reflection. Most people, however fastidious about cleanliness, have concealed spaces that are a complete mess.

These are generally areas that aren't frequently accessed. If these inaccessible areas are kept sparkling clean too, the person is most often suffering from a deep seated anxiety of nervousness disorder. These people are generally control freaks who are obsessed with the idea of controlling things around them to an unhealthy level.

Research also reveals that a disorganized, chaotic and unclean environment indicates creativity and innovativeness. People living or working in such messy and disorganized conditions tend to generate forward-thinking, resourceful and path-breaking solutions. Yes, the cliché about a scientist, writer or artist sporting a messier look and unkempt hair may actually be true from a personality-psychological angle.

Colors

What do colors within a person's immediate space reveal about him or her? The first thing that people probably look at when they enter someone's home or office is the color scheme used to do up the space. Bright, dazzling and bold colors instantly draw our attention to the space, while cool colors create a softer and more tranquil atmosphere. An individual's color choice can demonstrate a lot about their personality. For example, if the person has an inherent penchant or bold and vivid colors like red, purple, orange, magenta etc., they may be more adventurous, experimental and risk taking by nature. They aren't shy about expressing their thoughts and are constantly seeking new experiences. It signifies an outgoing, gregarious, unafraid and bold personality. These people aren't afraid to call a spade a spade.

On the other hand, people opting for cooler and more subtle shades may be reflective, quiet, restrained and analytical by nature. They are generally deep thinkers, who do not make hasty decisions. Their decisions are made after considering all possible options.

People who are inward focused will most likely have their homes done up in soft, subtle and solid hues, marked by muted patterns. Extroverts, on the other hand, tend to opt for more old, vibrant and experimental prints. Since they are more social and gregarious by nature, there is an inherent need to impress people. Extroverts are more outwardly focused, which means their decisions are more determined by what they think will please people around them.

Introverts seldom display this need to impress others and will often downplay themselves and their surroundings in a bid to avoid being noticed. Unlike extroverts, they are uncomfortable at the prospect of being the center of attention.

Prints and Designs

It may sound funny (or intriguing if you are like me). However, the prints or designs used to do up a person's home or office décor, or even their attire can be very telling about their personality. For example, bright, bold, large and vibrant prints can signify an uninhibited personality that is more self-assured, opinionated and seldom overwhelmed by other people's opinion. These people are fiercely original in their thoughts, opinions and actions.

They often have their own opinion on multiple issues and are rarely influenced by the thoughts, opinions and ideas of other people.

Likewise, quirky prints such as graffiti, pop art, animal motifs and polka dots can reveal a penchant for fun and creativity. It is an indication of a creative, independent thinking and original personality. The person isn't afraid to express themselves and is least concerned about fitting in with the crowd. They yearn to stand out rather than fit in. These are your path-breakers, rebels and trend-setters.

Geometric prints can demonstrate an inclination towards order, symmetry and organization. People who wear a lot of geometric prints or have their homes/offices done up in predominantly geometric prints may reveal an affinity for balance, orderliness and analysis. There is a deep-seated need to have everything in order.

In an interesting study conducted by Yale researchers, it was revealed that people who spend hours taking showers or in the bath are generally lonely or emotionally deprived people who seek warmth from the bath to compensate for the emotional warmth in their lives. Makes sense, doesn't it?

Do you a wall filled with motivational quotes and inspiring messages in your home or office? You may want to read this then. Psychologists have researched that people having a wall filled with inspirational quotes and messages are more often than not possess neurotic tendencies. These people utilize their environment or the space around them for soothing their nerves and helping them navigate the storms in their life. Of course, don't automatically assume that something is not quite normal about a person when you spot a wall filled with motivational posters. The best way to gather more clues is to talk to the person. Observe verbal and non-verbal clues carefully to gain deeper insights into their personality.

Old Stuff

Ever noticed how some people's homes resemble a junkyard because they store all the old and unwanted stuff? There are old uniforms, sports jerseys they've long outgrown, clothes that don't fit them any longer and other memorabilia that has no place in their current lives. These are most likely folks who are unable to discard their past and move on. They are unable to let go of the past and move ahead. There is a need to cling on to the past and a refusal to look into the future. Hoarding objects may mean that they are still emotionally connected with memories attached to these belongings.

For example, if you are still holding on to a dress that you've long outgrown because it was gifted to you by a former lover, you are probably unwilling to come to terms with the fact that the relationship is over. You are still emotionally clinging on to the relationship instead of moving on and looking into the future. There is a tendency to be closely attached to people and memories that these objects represent at a subconscious level.

Chapter 4:

Judging A Book By Its Cover

When you walk into a book store, how do you judge which book to pick up and which to pass? If you are like me, you are guilty of picking up books that have fancy titles, attractive covers and lots of visually arresting features. Accuse me of being shallow, but I also look at the quality of paper. Yes, judging a book by its cover is something we've all done at some point or the other.

We've all been fed on the belief that judging a book by its cover is not the right way to do it. However in a time and attention pressed world, where we rarely have the time to read people comprehensively, we seldom have an option but to analyze and speed people to make quick decisions about them. Reading a book by its cover or speed reading people may not be such a bad thing in today's times. People's outer appearances can often help you make solid and reliable conclusions about their personality. The subconscious visual that you form about an individual through their appearance is often accurate.

I know plenty of psychologists who believe that making snap judgments about people based on their appearances is an extremely narrow way of looking at it. However, the way a person treats himself or herself just as he/she treats his/her immediate environment can reveal a lot about their inherent personality. It can help you a gain a deeper understanding of their personality to make the communication even more meaningful.

The way a person dresses or maintains their outer appearance can reveal a lot about their internal feelings. Their exterior can often be a near accurate indicator of their thoughts, emotions and feelings. Ever noticed how when you are completely dejected or sad, you don't bother about how your hair or face looks? You don't have the inclination or zest to look good.

Similarly, when you are feeling more positive and upbeat, you will invest extra effort in looking good and feeling wonderful about yourself. People are well-dresses or sport a neatly-groomed appearance to gain respect or validation from others. They may want people to perceive them in a more positive light. It can also be a sign of high self-confidence, power and authority. People in positions of power and authority may also be wealthy, which gives them the resources to be expensively dressed and groomed. It can be a sign of influence, power and confidence. These folks are viewed in a more positive or flattering light by other people.

Here are some tips for reading people through their cover or outer appearance to make a near-accurate analysis of their personality or behavioral characteristics.

Good Influencers and Negotiators

Imagine a scenario where a plain looking person is selling you something you don't really need. He/she is plain looking and not very attractively dressed or groomed. Would you buy from him or her? The person doesn't appear like they are in a commanding or influential position when it comes to negotiations.

Now imagine another scenario where an extremely attractive, well-dressed and nattily groomed salesperson walks up to you and introduces themselves to you. Again, you don't really need what they are selling but you still listen to everything because the person is cute-looking, friendly and speaks with oodles of charm. By the end of their sales pitch, you realize that you can, in fact, use the product they are selling.

Attractive and well-groomed people have the power to influence people's decisions, however hollow it may seem. Of course, it isn't simply about wearing good clothes and looking good and ignoring everything else. There is a natural confidence and ease with which these people operate. Other factors such as friendliness, conversational skills, intelligence and other things matter too. This should explain why some people invest a bomb in maintaining their wardrobes and appearance.

Introverts and Extroverts

Extroverts thrive on adventure, new experiences, and risks. Their brains process dopamine starkly differently than it is processed in a person who is more inward driven or introverted. These thrill seekers think fast, act faster and are prone to be more impulsive when it comes to decision making. They will move and walk fast, which means they are at a greater risk of injuries.

This can be slightly stretched to conclude that people who have more injury scars or casts have higher chances of being extroverts. Their thrill seeking disposition and brain makes them more prone to accidents and injuries. Yes, these are the people who won't think twice before jumping out of a window to escape an adulterous confrontation.

Similarly, while introverts are more likely to observe your shoes and look at your feet while talking, extroverts will look you directly in the eyes while speaking. Since introverts are more inward driven and reflect upon their options before making a decision, they tend to seize/observe people. There is a tendency to look down at a person's feet because of the awkwardness involved in looking away from a person while speaking rather than looking into their eyes. To avoid this uncomfortable situation of looking everywhere around the eyes, introverts will glance at a person's shoes or feet while thinking.

Since extroverts are more outward driven and focused, they will look people in the eyes while talking. There is a tendency to experience rather than think, which means all their efforts are directed towards experiencing or listening to people instead of thinking about what people are talking. They'll seldom look in different directions (unless they are lying or there's another clear reason for the mismatch in behavior) and will have their eyes firmly fixated on the person they are speaking to.

Blue eyes and light, blonde hair has almost always been closely linked with extroversion. However, there isn't a conclusive study to support this view. More than anything, it is a popularly peddled media notion that is completely supported by the Hollywood and Disney brigade.

There is a definite bias towards light eyes and hair each time a character has to be represented as an extrovert. Ariel, Belle and Hercules are all Disney characters who've been portrayed as introverts with light hair and eyes. Today, you can't go about judging people's personality through the color of their eyes or hair because people are dying their hair and changing colored contact lenses faster than you can say personality.

Reading People Through Their Attire

Like we discussed earlier, the manner in which a person dresses reveals a lot about their personality. Neatly dressed and groomed people may have an inherent need to be respected and accepted within their social group. They may have a deep need to fit in or be validated by others. At times, dressing excessively well or paying too much attention to one's appearance can be a sign of narcissism of self-obsession. The person may also be suffering from a deeply rooted inferiority complex or low self-esteem that they are trying to compensate for by dressing well.

Sometimes, people who pay too much attention to their grooming and appearance may believe that they aren't good enough for anything and may use their looks to cover up for the perceived inadequacies in their life.

One of my friends could never match up to her older sibling when it came to intelligence, social skills and talent. While the parents lavishly praised her older sister for being an intelligent and talent student, she (the younger sibling) wasn't believed to be striking or extra ordinary in anything. Throughout her growing up years, she believed she wasn't good at anything and sought constant validation from people through her looks and clothes. She became obsessed with her appearance and spent huge sums of money on grooming, beauty products, beauty treatments and makeovers.

Thus, an excessive need to look good and dress well can also be a clue to an inferiority complex marked personality. Know more about a person before you make snap judgments about their outer appearance. However, appearance along with other non-verbal clues can offer you plenty of insights into an individual's subconscious thoughts, feelings and preferences.

Chapter 5:

Speed Reading People Through Their Photographs

There's no escaping people's pictures in the age of a constantly buzzing social media feed. Like it or hate it, people are going to pictures of themselves. However, the good news from the perspective of a person analyzer is you can gather plenty of clues for speed reading people even before you meet them simply by learning to read their photographs.

Imagine gaining some clues about a prospective employee before they come down for a face or face interview or learning more about a client before negotiating an important deal with them. How about picking the right date by gathering insights about his or her personality through their social media images? Every image of a person holds a fascinating amount of information, meaning, and an indication of his or her emotional state. We only have to be perceptive enough to watch out for these clues. Sometimes, we are so overcome by the aesthetics of the image or the photography that we completely miss the emotions behind the image.

This chapter attempts to offer you some insights about how people's photographs can be used for interpreting their values, personality and behavioral traits. There are some obvious and some subtle pointers about decoding an individual's personality through their photos. You'll learn to find more meaning and context within the images rather than viewing them as random shots.

Don't Be in a Rush

Since photographs capture moments where time freezes, you need to study the image carefully to avoid any biases or inaccurate readings about something that may have happened in a microsecond. This may be contrary to the fast-speed, short span of attention, limited energy and the multi-tasking disposition we display. Hit the brain's pause button, do some deep breathing and get yourself into slow motion before you begin analyzing people through their images. You need to approach the art of analyzing people with both curiosity and compassion.

Don't leave out any details Look at the entire image. What is it that holds your attention when you first look at the picture? What are the conspicuous aspects of the image? Slowly move your attention and awareness to the other parts of the images. Look at it from different angles and perspectives.

Pull the image closer to your vision to detect elements that would otherwise go unnoticed. There are plenty of subtle details that your eye may miss if you don't view it closely. Turning the image upside down or sideways allows you to view it from an unusual perspective, which can change your entire view point about the image. You'll end up noticing things you wouldn't have otherwise noticed.

Subjective Reactions

What is it that strikes you the most about an image when you see it for the first time? What emotions, feelings, thoughts and sensations overcome your mind when you look at the image on an instinctive level? Think of a single descriptive word or phrase as a caption or title for the image that captures your spontaneous reaction to the image.

Do you think the picture represents pride, anger, anxiety, relief, frustration, confinement, exhaustion, success, elation, exhilaration, smoothness, rage, sadness and other compelling emotions? Your gut level reaction offers a clue on what you are thinking about the person.

While observing or analyzing people through their photographs, one of the most important considerations is your instant or an immediate reaction. However, you'll need to go beyond the first impression. You'll have to apply some amount of free association to analyze the person. Through free association, you are focusing on all elements of the image. Here are some questions you can ask yourself to facilitate greater free association to analyze people through images.

What does the picture remind you of?

What is the predominant emotion expressed by the person in the image?

What memories, incidents and experiences can you pull out from your own state of awareness on looking at the image?

How would you title the image?

However, when you are analyzing people through their pictures, beware against what psychologists terms projection. Projection is an unconscious process through which our own feelings, emotions, experiences and memories distort our perception of other people we are analyzing. You may invariably end up projecting your own feelings and experiences to them than trying to identify their personality. This is especially true for more ambiguous images. You don't know if you are rightly empathizing with people /reading them correctly or simply recalling your own experiences.

Sometimes, our own subjective reactions get in the way of reading people accurately. However, overcome this tricky situation and identifying when your own experiences and biases are getting in the way of analyzing people will help you be a more effective people analyzer.

Facial expressions

Human beings are innately expressive when it comes to tuning in to other people's facial expressions. What is your first reaction on looking at the person's face in the photograph? Psychologists have recognized seven basic emotions in a person – surprise, contempt, fear, sadness, anger, disgust and happiness. Keep these seven basic emotions in mind while analyzing people's expressions in images. At times, the expressions are underplayed or subtle, which makes it challenging to pin down the basic emotion.

Look for pictures where the person may not be aware that they are being clicked since that can be a more accurate representation of their subconscious mind.

Relationships

Again, you can tell a lot about the relationship between people by looking at their photographs. If a person is leaning in the direction of another person, there may be attraction or affection between the people. Similarly, if people are leaning in the opposite direction from each other, the relationship may lack warmth. If you notice a person clinging on to their partner's arm in almost every photograph, he or she may most likely be insecure about losing their partner. It may reveal a deep sense of insecurity or fear of losing their partner.

Try to predict the relationship between people through their body language in images. This can also be done in any public place where you have some time on hand to check people's body language, relationship equation and reactions. What are their feelings, emotions, thoughts and attitudes towards each other? Is there a pattern in the manner through which people touch, lean towards each other or look at one another? Does their body language reveal a lack of connectedness?

One of my favorite pastimes when it comes to analyzing people is looking at the photographs of celebrity couples and trying to read the nature of their relationship and/or their personality through their body language and expressions. I try to analyze if the image reveals intimacy, affection and positivity? Or it demonstrates tension, disharmony and conflict? Akeret, a well-known psychologist, believes that a photograph can also predict a relationships' future.

Some signs of comfort include smiling, holding hands, titling head in the direction of their partner.

Hip to hip posture may indicate things are going great between the couple. How is the palmer touch? If it is touching with the full hand, the partners are close and affectionate. On the other hand, finger tips or fist touching can be a sign of being distant and reserved. Crossing legs may mean that they weren't very comfortable or open at the time the picture was taken. If you find a person crossing their arms or legs in almost every photograph, they may be suspicious, doubtful, cynical and unenthusiastic by nature.

Profile Pictures and Personality Traits

A big body of research suggests that human beings have the tendency to assess one another's personality through a quick glimpse. This is exactly why first impressions are so lasting. It takes us only 3-4 seconds to form an impression about a person through their verbal and non-verbal clues. Sometimes, they may not even say anything and we can subconsciously tune in to personality.

A recent research study reveals that you don't even have to meet a person once to form an opinion about him or her. All you need is a quick glance at their Facebook or even Tinder profile picture to gauge their personality. Here are the big five personality traits that are revealed through a person's profile picture.

The big five is pretty much the same as a scientific classification of personalities as Briggs-Myers is for recruitment. This personality approach classifies personalities on the basis of five fundamental traits, namely – introversion-extroversion, agreeableness, open to new experiences, conscientiousness and neuroticism.

A quick glance at your social media profile picture is sufficient for you to rate people correctly on the five fundamental dimensions. In a research conducted by PsyBlog, it was observed through a scientific analysis of the profile pictures of thousands of social media participant personalities that there were very specific and consistent patterns when it came to each of the five personality attributes.

For example, people scoring high on conscientiousness used images that were natural, filter-free, bright and vibrant. They were not afraid to express a large number of emotions through their pictures. If fact they displayed a higher number of emotions through their images than all other personality types.

You'll also find people scoring high on openness taking the most amazing shots. They are creative, innovative and resourceful. They'll play a lot with applications and filters owing to their creativity. Their pictures will be more artistic, unique and feature greater contrasts. Generally, people who score high on openness have their face occupy more space than any other feature in the photograph.

Extraversion folks will have perpetually broad smiles plastered on their faces. They will use collages and may surround their profile picture with used vibrant images. On the other hand, simple images with very little color or brightness is a strong indication of neuroticism. These pictures are likely to display a blank expression or in extreme cases may even conceal their face, according to the blog.

Agreeable people may often seem to the nicest people to get along with among all personality types. However turns out, they aren't really great photographers. Agreeable people are known to post unflattering images of themselves! However, even with the poor or unflattering images of themselves, they will be seen smiling or displaying a positive expression. The images will be vibrant, positive and lively.

Chapter 6:

Spotting Deception Through Non-Verbal Clues

When people used to ask me during fun games what is what one superpower I would like to develop, I would always say the ability to spot liars and cheats. No, I didn't have any super detective or FBI aspirations! All I wanted to do was equip myself to be able to determine when people are lying and when they are telling the truth because this can save us plenty of heartbreak, relationship trouble, deals gone wrong and soured social relationships. If there's one superpower that can save you a lot of troubles and conflict, it is the ability to spot lies.

Though we can identify liars on an instinctive level, there are some clear verbal and non-verbal techniques that help you identify deception and lies.

Our unconscious or subconscious mind is capable of detecting liars fairly quickly and accurately.

Fortunately, liars offer tons of signals through their words, voice and body language that can be quickly caught by an expert people analyzer. Here are some top tips for making you the ultimate lie detector.

1. Jerky Head Movements

People who aren't speaking the truth of trying to deceive others make sudden, unexpected and erratic head movements when they are confronted with a question. The head will retract slightly and move in a jerkier manner. In some cases, it may tilt a little. This happens in split seconds just before the person begins to reply to your question.

2. Direction of Eye Movements

When someone is lying, their eyes will generally move towards their right side. The eyes will go up, and then towards the right. This implies that the person is making up information. Since specific functions are performed by certain parts of our brain, the direction in which a person's eyes move can determine the function performed by their brain.

For example, when a person's eyes move to the upper left, we are most likely trying to recall information that is stored in the memory which means the person may be telling the truth. However, if a person's eyes move to the upper right, he or she isn't trying to recall or extract information from the memory. They are making up information or lying. When you confront someone with a question, their eye movements will reveal a lot about whether they are lying or speaking the truth. The reverse of this true for left –handed people.

In left-handed people, if the person looks to their upper right while thinking, they are trying to recall information from their memory. However, when they look at the upper left direction when confronted with a question, they are most likely making up facts or misleading you.

So before you term someone a liar, pleas ensure you know if the person is left or right handed.

Not just the direction of a person's eyes but also movements such as raising eyebrows or widening eyes is a non-verbal signal of deceit. People often look try to look stunned when their lies are called out. In a bid to appear surprised and shocked by your insinuation, they may widen their eyes or raise their eyebrows. It may be an act to make another feel guilty about accusing them.

3. The Projection Technique

Liars are brilliant at employing the projection technique. When confronted with a question, they will most likely come up with a counter question after pausing for a while. This is a typical response of liars. They will pause for a while to buy time and contemplate their response to being confronted.

This will be followed by an accusatory question directed towards you such as "Do you think I am a liar?" or "How can you accuse me of being a liar?" or "Why were you snooping around?" and similar other accusatory questions that are specifically designed to make you feel guilty about confronting them.

4. Nervousness

However smart deceivers think they are, they offer plenty of clues through their verbal and non-verbal communication. Watch out for their leg and feet movements because that is one of the most neglected parts of the body while we are interacting or communicating with people.

Liars can manipulate other signals such as maintaining eye contact or keeping a relaxed posture, since the fact that people who are speaking the truth always look you in the eye is now common and widely shared knowledge. They know that looking into a person's eyes while speaking can make them come across as more truthful.

However, some signals such as faking their leg or feet movements don't happen too effectively since these aren't very visible or noticeable areas of the body. This makes manipulating leg or feet movements near impossible. Plus it happens at such a subconscious level that it is near impossible to fake. When people lie or try to mislead others, their legs (or even feet) start twitching slightly. They may be fidgeting with their clothes or pretend to brush off lint from their shoulders.

Shrugging or slouching are other obvious signs of a liar.

5. Watch Out For Verbal Signals

While non-verbal signals can reveal a lot about whether a person is lying or telling the truth, his or her words can also be extremely revealing. People who are lying generally speak using a slower and more spaced out way. There are plenty of pauses that they use for buying time.

Their speech will most likely have a more uneven or inconsistent pitch. Liars will be more hesitant in the way they speak. Genuine people answer quickly, while false responses come up only after careful consideration of all options. The person will take more time to deliberate, which will slow their speech. It takes time to think of appropriate words when you are lying.

Also, people who lie or mislead others have the tendency to detach themselves from the situation. They will deny any responsibility or detach from the occurrence, which simply means they'll use lesser sentences in the active voice.

They will seldom use sentences that begin with "I" and will often use passive voice or speak in a manner that something happened to them rather than they did something. Liars will either offer very little details or a lot of details in a bid to cover the fact that they are lying. There is a tendency will volunteer with plenty of unnecessary details. They'll attempt to throw your questioning in another direction by offering a lot of details, most of which may be irrelevant, just to demonstrate that they are speaking the truth. They hope people will buy their 'innocence' if they give long and elaborate answers.

This makes liars use plenty of fluff words and filler and very little concrete details. They won't offer solid information. Their sentences will be long and yet not offer anything substantial. People who are lying with almost always never offer tiny and verifiable details. They will focus more on emotions or how hurt they are or how someone is feeling. The conversation or interaction will be more fraught with an apparent show of emotions rather than verifiable facts. Always confront a liar by asking them specifics, which only someone who us speaking the truth would know.

Even when you spot a clear contradiction in what they are saying and what you know is the truth, let them continue speaking. Give the confidence that you trust their version of what happened and allow them to give you even more clues of their lie. This can be used for confronting them at a later date. Let them go on and on with stories and created versions that will eventually help nail them. The idea is to catch them in their own spun web!

Liars will almost always detach themselves from an occurrence or event and focus on the other person or people. They will rarely use "I" or "me" while constructing their sentences since they are attempting to detach themselves from their falsehood at a subconscious level. They are not recollecting facts from their mind. Rather they are fabricating lies, which is why they are trying to distance themselves from their version of events. It happens at a very subtle and subconscious level, and they are obviously not aware of it (until they read this book that is!). There is a very strong need to psychologically distance or detach themselves from the situation

6. Physiological Effects

Lying produces plenty of psychological effects within the human body (which is what is captured by lie detecting machines) such as immediate blood vessels swelling, rapid heart rate, increases palpitations, sweating, itchy reaction on the skin and much more. When out blood vessels expand or experience swelling, the skin invariably begins to feel scratchy. This is why liars start feeling uncontrollably itchy when they lie. The itchy nose may not be such a myth after all and may have a deep physiological significance when it comes to spotting liars.

7. The Face Touch

The way in which a person touches their face demonstrates whether he or she is lying or speaking the truth. People who are lying will more often than not cover their mouth using their hands. This is a subconscious gesture to prevent spilling out information that they shouldn't or a way for them to suppress the urge of blurting out the truth. When people cover the mouth with their hands, the thumb will most likely be near the cheeks. Some fingers will be spread over the mouth to psychologically cover up.

Another sign of deception is when liars are confronted with the truth or a question and instead of answering the question; they break into a fake cough bout. This is nothing more than an attempt to buy time for making up tales.

8. How Are the Hands Positioned?

Keeping their hands at the back can be a sign of trying to conceal something. Liars will seldom reveal their palms or make an open palm gesture. People who are transparent, genuine and speaking the truth will keep their palms wide open, while those who are being deceitful or lying will turn their palms upside down.

It is a subconscious gesture that they have something to hide. Liars will often place their palms in their pocket to avoid revealing them to the other person, which is a near accurate indication of them wanting to conceal facts.

9. The Voice Raise

When a person's voice rises slightly or starts becoming shakier owing to muscle contraction, the person may be undergoing some form of stress. Their voice inflection may be higher than normal, and there may be palpable tension within the voice. An expert people reader will not miss these clues.

10. Variance in Confidence

Carefully observe the variation in a person's confidence when they are confronted with a question or the truth. They may either freeze or become extremely verbose, thus revealing lack of confidence or control. If you want to get the person to giveaway more clues about their lies and deceit, employ a technique used by investigators. Rather than making the communication appear like an interrogation, make it more conversational.

Liars more often than not give themselves away completely by being more illogical, sporadic and erratic in their responses. If you interact with them in a more conversation manner by letting their guard down, they will invariably give themselves away.

11. Look At A Person's Shoulders

Sometimes, a person's shoulders diminish or close in while lying. This is the exact opposite of an expanding posture, which indicates power, authority and self-confidence. By closing in their shoulders, the person is trying to diminish their posture because subconsciously and consciously too they are aware that they did something shameful, which reduces them in stature.

When they know they have done something wrong, the person's confidence invariably reduces. They are almost ashamed of their act, which leads them to form a more diminutive or reduced posture. Liars often conduct themselves with greater vulnerability. There is always a fear and insecurity that their lies will be caught, which leads them to hunching posture. When the elbows draw closer together, the individual takes on a posture that makes them look more diminutive in size, which is a sign of low confidence or vulnerability.

12. Microexpressions

Microexpressions occur in split seconds, which make them tough to fake. It is near impossible to work on or manipulate one's microexpressions even if people can mislead with their regular facial expressions. These happen so fast that there's no way a person can modify them unless he or she is a practiced manipulator who is aware of body language manipulation techniques. Laypeople, however, will seldom be able to fake microexpressions.

When a person isn't speaking the truth, their mouth will become slightly skewed. The eyes will subtly roll right after the person has spoken a lie. This is a near accurate microexpression of spotting deception. Other not so obvious microexpressions are a change in the color of an individual's cheeks, expanded nostrils, increased sweating, lip biting, and quick eye movements in all directions. These are nothing but signals of brain activity when a liar is processing information that isn't true. There are certain reactions in the brain based on the activity that is happening within it. These processes or reactions are closely connected with movements on the face or physiological facial reactions, which leads to microexpressions.

13. Pose Non-Threatening Questions

One of the best ways for identifying if a person is telling the truth is by posing more neutral and seemingly non-threatening questions. The idea is to get people to shed their guard and open up when you begin asking them questions.

Begin by establishing a baseline for the person's behavior. How does he or she normally behave? What is his or her predominant personality type? Then compare and contrast their current behavior with how they normally behave. Do you spot a clear mismatch? Start by engaging in small talk about the weather, hobbies, passions, weekend plans and other similar topics. Get them in a more relaxed, unguarded and normal state of mind! This will allow them to drop their guard and answer in a more relaxed manner.

Now closely observe their movements, expressions, eye movements, gestures, feet, posture and other non-verbal clues while they are speaking. Is the person looking directly into your eyes while speaking? Are they constantly shifting their gaze? Pose sufficient queries to establish a pattern.

My favorite technique when it comes to establishing a baseline behavior is asking them questions they are comfortable with and observe their body language. Note as much information as you can about their body language for this will give you a fairly good idea about their baseline or normal body language when they are comfortable discussing the topic at hand. Then gently shift to a topic that makes them uncomfortable or confront them with questions related to their lies.

Note any variance in the body language. Is there a clear mismatch in their body language from what it was when they were comfortable talking about a subject? Do they suddenly display feelings or discomfort or vulnerability? If there is a mismatch when you become more confrontational, they may have something to hide. If their body language suddenly changes when they are confronted, you may have to put pieces of the picture together to call out their lies.

Chapter 7:

The Attraction Body Language

You may be insanely attracted to a person but may not have the courage to ask them out owing to the prospect of facing humiliation and rejection. Imagine how easier things would be if you knew if they are as much into you as you are into them. Think of a situation where you've been set up on a blind date by enthusiastic friends or you find a date online, and really want to know if they are attracted to you. You may go out on a first date and come back not knowing whether the person really liked you or not!

Wouldn't it be nice if there could be a telepathic way to gauge if a person feels truly attracted towards you? How can you figure out if a person is genuinely attracted to you or is being plain nice to you because they don't want to hurt you (yes, we've all been guilty of this)?

Can verbal and non-verbal clues help you establish a potential lover's true feelings, emotions, thoughts and intentions? Can body language be used for unlocking a person's subconscious mind to tune in to their innermost feelings and thoughts about you? Use these secret attraction clues (that I rarely share with anyone) to help you gain increases social proof and experience more gratifying and fulfilling relationships.

The Attraction Signals

When an individual is attracted to you, they will transmit plenty of feel good or positive non-verbal clues for you to tune in to at a subconscious level. To begin with, when a person is deeply attracted to you, their body will almost always face you.

Everything from their face to their chest, shoulders and feet will most likely be pointed in your direction. The person will lean closer while speaking or interacting with you in a bid to get closer on a subconscious and emotional level. When

185

they stand at a distance of under four feet away from you, they are keen on entering or personal space or inner circle of friends. They are trying to physically enter your inner zone or personal space to make a place for themselves in it.

If you want to know if a person is keenly into you or interested in you, don't give in to their interest straightaway. Rather than facing them, maintain a shoulder to shoulder position. If they person is truly interested in you, he or she will make an effort to win your attraction. Let them know that they've to win your attraction for you to stand facing them or mirror their attraction signals.

Leaning in the direction of a person is almost always a sign of attraction. We subconsciously lean towards people we are attracted to. When a person leans towards you in a group, it is clear that they are interested in you (or what you are speaking). Of course, sometimes a person may be simply keen on listening to what you are saying, in which case you will have to look at other clues. However, leaning towards a person within a group setting is a subconscious indication that they are drawn towards you.

Another sign of attraction includes seizing a person from up to down, and then down to up. This is a primitive way (which is still alive) for checking out the sexual potential of a prospective mate.

Together with other clues, uncrossed arms and legs can be a sign of attraction. Similarly, a broad smile dilated pupils and open palms can also reveal attraction. Head tilting is another sign of interest and engagement. It signals a person's desire to communicate to you that they are always around for you. Looking at a person in the eye for long while speaking can also be a huge sign of attraction. If you are attracted to a person or want to win their affection, avoid looking over their head or even all over the place. It reveals lack of interest and sensitivity, which will not give them the right signal.

Touch

Touch is a clue that an individual is completely comfortable in your presence. They may also be keen or getting to know more about you. They may get flirtatious or hit on you by playfully touching you. Some of the most common initial attractions signals are placing their hand over your hand, brushing their shoulder or leg against your shoulder or leg while talking to you and pretending to touch you accidently.

If you are confused about how to read a person's touches, observe how they touch another person versus how they touch you. If they are generally touchy-feely with everyone around, it is their baseline personality. However, if they make special exceptions in the manner in which they you, it is more often than not a sign of attraction. If the individual touches more than normal or in a different way, he or she may be attracted to you.

If you are attracted to a person, use body language to your advantage by conveying your feelings through non-verbal signals. Don't distance yourself from the person even if you don't want to send out very obvious signs of attraction. On a subconscious level, they may not realize they are attracted to you. Similarly, don't go all out and make the person step back in discomfort. Maintain a balance. Start with a light or playful tap on the shoulder or elbows. It is harmless yet reveals that a person likes you. Then gradually, move to touching their arm, wrist or back while talking. Make the touch more gradual and subtle so they don't wince or retreat with discomfort.

Mirroring

Mirroring happens at a deeply subconscious level and is one of the most reliable signals of a person's attraction. Watch out for people mirroring your actions. There is either a deeply seated need to be accepted or they are truly attracted to you. Sometimes after you've just met or been introduced to a person at a party, you'll notice that he or she starts mirroring everything from your words to your nods to your hand gestures to expressions.

People who don't know much about reading or analyzing people will often miss these clues. However, on a subconscious level, this is a sign that the person is seeking your acceptance or approval. When you are leaning against the bar, you'll notice a person come up to you and lean in the same position as you before striking up a conversation. They are doing nothing but attempting to mirror your actions in a bid to make you feel that they are one among your kind. People will hold their glass exactly in the manner in which you are holding yours or they may take a sip on their drink right after you do to show you that they are like you. The feeling of affiliating with people on a psychological level drives people to mirror their actions.

Conclusion

I sincerely hope it has offered you tons of proven strategies, tried and tested techniques and effective tips for reading people in multiple situations and life circumstances, while making you a perceptive people reader!

Whether you're trying to gauge what a potential client is thinking during a deal or if your hot new crush is attracted to you or if you want to hire perfect person for a role in your organization, this book presents a treasure casket of practical tips and wisdom nuggets to help you read people like books in varied situations. This, even with people who don't talk much because there are plenty of non-verbal clues!

The next step is to simply use this invaluable people reading handbook by implementing the strategies explained here in your everyday life. You aren't going to be an expert people reader overnight. It comes with lots of observation, consistency and practice.

Get into the habit of speed reading people using these strategies in several places from airports to bars to corporate boardrooms to cafes, when you have some free time at hand.

Finally, if you enjoyed reading the book, please take the time to share your thoughts by posting a review on Amazon. It'd be greatly appreciated.

Here's to being an awesome people reader, who can use the super power of analyzing people's thoughts, emotions and feelings to enjoy more rewarding and gratifying relationships.

How To Analyze People 3

Uncover Sherlock Holmes' Secrets To
Analyze Anyone On The Spot

-

Including DIY Exercises

Patrick Lightman

Introduction

The year was 1886. Arthur Conan Doyle was running a struggling surgery clinic in Portsmouth but had other preoccupations in mind. He wanted to write, and so write he did.

Deeply inspired by his mentor, Dr. Joseph Bell who could provide a near accurate - or in some cases - even a perfect diagnosis upon looking at a patient, Conan Doyle was fueled with imagination and creativity in the 3 weeks that it took to write his first ever Sherlock Holmes novel - *A Study in Scarlet*.

Following his incessant writing and sleepless nights, the proud doctor approached a handful of publishers, all of which turned their backs on his book and closed their doors. It wasn't until he was able to sell his book to the *Beeton's Christmas Annual* that his book received *some* publicity.

The *Beeton's Christmas Annual* at the time contained *A Study in Scarlet,* and two original drawing room plays, all buried together in a sea of advertisements. The year was 1887, and the paperback magazine sold out before Christmas at the cost of 1 shilling per copy.

While the rapid sales would have you assume that Conan Doyle probably met success shortly after that year's Christmas, he didn't. The physician-turned-author was quoted saying that "the book had no particular success at the time", a truth that was proven by the general lack of interest in both Arthur and his eccentric detective character.

When he sold *A Study in Scarlet* to Beeton's, he was offered no more than £25 for the copyright. Initially, the doctor tried to argue and bargain. But due to the lack of offers and interest in his book, he had no choice but to agree to the deal.

Sad as it may seem, the now iconic author earned nothing more than that initial £25 on his first ever Holmes masterpiece which today sells roughly $20 a copy and is often considered a vintage classic. Even as the initial novel gained popularity as Sherlock Holmes became more prominent throughout the years, Conan Doyle saw no royalties since he sold the copyright entirely.

At the time, it seems people weren't as interested in the intellectual exploits of Sherlock Holmes, and perhaps his unconventional behavior and investigative work flew over their heads.

But as time went on, more and more people started to pick up on Sherlock's astounding detective prowess, turning both Conan Doyle and his character into a success after 1890 when the second installment of the series was published.

Although it didn't quite receive the acclaim that Conan Doyle had hoped, details in *A Study in Scarlet* established the kind of character Sherlock was and the skills he possessed that would make him iconic in pop culture 130 years down the line.

His disdain for social mores, his remarkable fastidiousness, his habit of selecting only interesting cases, and his exemplary capacity to accurately profile any person at a glance all made him the most filmed fictional human character since the advent of cinematic film. This, and of course, one of the most popular idols for people who want to make use of their mind in the most efficient ways possible.

Flashing back to *A Study in Scarlet* when Holmes first meets Watson, we're given a glimpse as to how impressive the super sleuth actually is when it comes to deciphering people at a glance. With no more than one look, Sherlock tells his new acquaintance that he presumed the doctor had come from Afghanistan after serving in the war.

Was he correct? Absolutely. Did anyone tell him? Absolutely not. So how exactly did he come to infer such specific information? It all lies in his impeccable capacity to *analyze anyone on the spot*.

While very few of us are considered to be super sleuths in this modern day and age, there are countless benefits to learning *how* to read people. Giving us the capability to call the right shots, make the right move, and avoid confrontation all before it happens, learning to analyze people upon meeting them can improve your relationship and help you become far more efficient at social interactions.

So, if you're tired of bickering over misunderstandings with friends and family, if you're sick of hearing your boss tell you that you've misinterpreted his instructions yet again, if you're hoping to make new friends, keep old ones, and experience a stress-free social life, then the answer might be right here.

Find out how you can turn Sherlock Holmes' master investigator capabilities into real-life skills that you can use in any social situation.

Chapter 1:

Inside The Mind Of Sherlock Holmes

"And these other people?"

"They are mostly sent on by private inquiry agencies. They are all people who are in trouble about something, and want a little enlightening. I listen to their story, they listen to my comments, and then I pocket my fee."

"But do you mean to say," I said, "that without leaving your room you can unravel some knot which other men can make nothing of, although they have seen every detail for themselves?"

"Quite so. I have a kind of intuition that way."

- Dialogue between Sherlock Holmes and John Watson, A Study in Scarlet

What made Sherlock such a success at his trade?

Why did established police officers and authorities come to him for guidance and assistance? Why was he the go-to name in London for anyone and everyone looking for answers - regardless of whether or not he was familiar with their particular situation?

In A Study in Scarlet, Sherlock tells Watson a little more about himself and his skill, and the doctor finds himself intrigued by the super sleuth's popularity as an investigator, leading him to believe that perhaps, the man's strange ethic did in fact hold some value.

Throughout the Sherlock Holmes series, we read about the master detective constantly surprising the good doctor with conclusions and inferences that seem to have come from nothing more than scant, often seemingly irrelevant evidence. This is what makes him popular, and this is what makes him a reliable professional in his respective field.

One other skill that came hand in hand with Sherlock's impeccable detective capabilities was his knack for deciphering people at a mere glance. He showcased this skill early on in the first novel, where he tells Watson - upon meeting for the first time - that he perceived the doctor had served in Afghanistan.

Having just met and not knowing much about each other aside from their names and their trade, Watson was baffled at how Holmes knew something so specific. For a while, the doctor was convinced that someone had told him of Watson's exploits serving in the Anglo-Afghan war.

Later on in the book, Sherlock explains that no one had told him anything. Instead, he simply took what he was based on the doctor's appearances and put the pieces together from there. Unnaturally dark skin, an injured arm, and a tired face to go with his stiff army doctor demeanor. Where else would the man have been other than Afghanistan, Sherlock surmised.

These days, there are very few people who can decode others at a glance the same way Holmes did.

In fact, with so many distractions, charades, styles, personalities, cultures, and influences working within and around us, it has become increasingly difficult to understand people at a glance.

But a first-time meet isn't the only time when these influences might work against us. Even in well-established relationships, misunderstandings occur because we *can't* completely grasp how others around us think, act, and behave. So we end up clashing with them, battling it out because we have our own perspectives.

If we could adapt Sherlock's skill for interpreting others and deciphering people at a glance, then we might be able to mitigate misunderstandings, miscommunication, and arguments across our social interactions.

So how do we do it? First let's take a look into the Sherlock Holmes method for socialization.

Clarity

One of the principles that Sherlock fervently believes in is the importance of silence when dealing with any situation. During his investigative work, he would often refrain from speaking, and would often be seen with his eyes closed and his fingers pressed against each other as if deep in thought. Why did he do this?

Sherlock believed that clarity of mind was an important facet of properly understanding a situation - or in other cases, people. Having a clutter-free mind that's prepared to take information without any interference from your own thoughts, ideas, and prejudices reduces noise and prevents misinterpretation.

Detachment

How can detachment help when it comes to social interactions? Shouldn't we be eager, willing, and excited to communicate, socialize, and participate in conversation and interaction if we want to properly understand the people around us? If that were the case, then perhaps Sherlock Holmes would have been far less talented at deciphering people at a glance.

Although it seems counterintuitive, the best way to actually understand a person is by detaching yourself from the interaction. This has something to do with clarity, and prevents your mind from labeling certain factors and interpreting them how you might be inclined to.

Consider this: you're a well-educated young professional and you've been looking for business partners to help you build and fund a small enterprise that you've been planning for a while. As you're having lunch one day, a man in a suit, looking polished and well-off, walks into the restaurant.

He sits at the table across from yours and orders nothing more than the most expensive wine on the restaurant's menu. He then pulls out his smartphone and calls up who you assume is his business partner. They're talking numbers.

With your limited knowledge of corporate talk, you figure that this man is minted and that he has funds to spare. In fact, it sounds like he might be looking to invest in a business idea just like yours.

Do you approach him? If you would, what would you say and how would you say it?

Now, before we dissect that scenario, consider this second situation. You've walked out of the restaurant after having your lunch and a teenager approaches you. You scan his appearance quickly and see that he's wearing raggedy old clothes, and it seems as though it's been a while since the last time he took a bath given the stench that's coming off of him.

He wants to talk to you about a monetary donation that he wants to use for his education. But as he talks, you notice what seem to be needle marks covering his forearm.

What do you do? Do you let him finish talking, and how do you deal with this particular person?

Most of those who read the first encounter would say that they'd put their best foot forward. This person was *exactly* the kind of funder and business mentor that you need, so it would be highly beneficial for you to be able to get on his good side. In the second situation however, you might not have been too kind. Some might say that they would have turned the teenager away because he was probably lying to fund an addiction.

But, did you notice something about these typical reactions? For the most part, we as humans have a tendency to react based on our *emotions*. How will this person benefit me? Is this someone I want to associate myself with? What will I gain out of engaging with this person?

Learning to detach the self from the situation and regarding a person without bias helps prevent you from acting in a way that leans towards your own egocentric tendencies. That's often how arguments and misunderstandings happen in the first place - because most of us are wired to look at a person and think, *how will this interaction benefit me?*

In some cases, attachment also occurs when it comes to the way we perceive ourselves. Some people feel that they should interact only with those that they feel fall within similar socioeconomic or cultural barriers. Anyone who *seems* to fall outside of those limits might be approached with caution, or not at all.

Observation

Once you're free from mental clutter and persona bias, it then becomes easier to observe in detail. Sherlock showcased his keen eye for observation multiple times throughout the series, which actually contributed greatly to his success and popularity.

For instance, in *The Hound of the Baskervilles*, he

revealed his thought process at the end of the novel, including the reason why one of Sr. Henry's boots had gone missing. He claimed that the first boot used in the investigation didn't work because the hounds couldn't get a scent off of it since it was brand new. This was also the reason why the other boots had gone missing as an attempt to hide evidence.

To anyone investigating the same case, the newness of the boot might not have been an object of interest. But for Sherlock, it became the turning point that ultimately led to the arrest.

Having this kind of keen eye for observation doesn't only help reveal truths about a situation, but may also shed light on how you should approach a new acquaintance. Taking notes on how a person is dressed, how they approach you, their body language, facial expressions, tone of voice, and virtually every aspect of their being before, during, and after an interaction can help you better understand how to deal with them.

Demeanor

There's no question that social interaction is just a series of reactions between people - even before they've actually engaged. Eye contact, posture, facial expressions - we all take these things into account without knowing it, and then fashion our approach and reactions based on what the other person is feeding us.

While previous discussions in this guide should have already taught you *not* to let someone else's demeanor dictate your reactions, it's equally important to make sure *you're* not doing anything to inhibit a person from being guarded. What does that mean?

Answer this question: Do you think a stranger would like to approach you or talk to you if you had your arms crossed over your chest, and your brows furrowed down the middle of your forehead? Probably not. If they did decide to talk to you, they might feel intimidated, or they might try to act with slight hostility and aggression to show you that your intimidation tactics don't work.

In any case, having the wrong demeanor could interfere with a person's real behavior, causing them to act a certain way as a response to your aura. This could interfere with your observations, and lead you to call the wrong shots later on.

Sherlock *knew* that his physical behavior could cause differences in the way the people around him would act, so he devised a way to make sure that his demeanor wouldn't get in the way of his efforts to collect evidence. That was, he would make sure that he would adopt an aura of neutrality, and depending on the case, he would lean slightly towards a slight irritability or slight concern.

Why? A neutral, open demeanor made people around him feel that they weren't being judged, so they didn't feel the need to act in a way that deflects his judgment. If you've read any of the Sherlock Holmes novels, you'll find that that's how he would often manage to get face to face with a perpetrator, allowing them to feel comfortable and unjudged in his presence, and encouraging them to speak and share their alibis as Holmes absorbed the information and pieced together his case.

In some cases, Holmes would be neutral yet mildly irritable, especially when dealing with people he only needed to deliver facts. Inspector Lestrade, for example, was a detective inspector who often asked Sherlock for his assistance whenever he would reach a dead end. Holmes had no fondness nor appreciation for Lestrade, and only really accepted his requests as he needed money.

So in many of their interactions, you'll find that Sherlock would often showcase slight irritability that made Lestrade provide him all the information he needed minus unnecessary pleasantries. In this instance, his demeanor would definitely still be useful, allowing him to get all the details of the case and making no room for interactions that might eat up time for no reason.

In certain cases, you might also find Sherlock acting with slight concern. This was often what he would do when dealing with private individuals that would seek him for assistance on the disappearance or death of a loved one. Over time, it would also be the way he would approach Watson who became a very close friend of his as the series progressed.

Chapter 2:

Understand Yourself First

"I'm not a psychopath. I'm a high functioning sociopath. Do your research."

- Sherlock Holmes, TV Series

If there's anything that Sherlock was an expert at, it was *knowing himself*. The super sleuth understood his own mind, and that made it easy for him to control himself, his thoughts, and his actions. Having full jurisdiction over his own cognition allowed the master investigator to make calculated decisions and quick however accurate calculations of *who people were* - all done in lightning speed.

Being able to *know yourself* is an essential step in the entire process of learning about others. Knowing your own personality type, decoding your tendencies when faced with social interactions, and learning how to alter your own demeanor to encourage outsiders to approach, talk, and act unguarded are important facets of becoming an expert at decoding those around you.

What's Your Social Personality Type?

First of all, it's important to know what your social personality type is. While there are a variety of tests that you can take online to give you a *label* to go with your usual socialization trends, there is no better way to truly grasp how you are as a social creature than by *metacognition*.

It takes a lot of mindfulness to be able to *think* about the way you *think*, especially during social interaction. But in doing so, you can unlock some realities that might not have seemed apparent at the start. To begin the process, try asking yourself these questions:

1. When was the last time I argued with someone? What were the sequence of events

that led to the rift? Did I show any behaviors that might have aggravated the situation? How could I have improved the outcomes of our interaction?

2. Who do I consider my closest or best friend? How did I meet this person? What might this individual appreciate about the way I interact with him or her?

3. When faced with a stranger, what is my initial reaction? How do I choose to present myself? Am I talkative and overbearing, taking control of the conversation from the start? Or do I prefer to let the stranger lead?

4. Are there times when I feel compelled to engage in interaction, or to completely avoid it? When does this happen and why do I sometimes feel that way?

Now that you know the answers to these questions, you might already have some sort of understanding of your socialization trend. Some might have found themselves to be particularly friendly even with strangers, others might be more standoffish or intimidating. Whatever the case, it's highly probable that your social personality *isn't the ideal* one for decoding strangers.

The purpose of this exercise wasn't exactly to help you put a name on your socialization trend, but rather to teach you *how to ask yourself the right questions* in order to audit your own personality. Knowing how to think about and process the way you engage with others can shed light on errors in your approach and provide you feedback that you can use to become more efficient in future encounters.

The next time you find yourself in a social interaction gone-wrong, take a moment to trace back your steps. What happened? Where did the conversation turn sour? And what can you do now to try to neutralize the situation and avoid confrontation?

Asking yourself these questions even in the middle

of an argument should help you reflect on your behavior at that given moment. It also helps to reflect on previous confrontations you might have had. Taking the time to understand how things might have gone wrong in the past will help you avoid the same mistakes in the future. This way, you can have a more polished approach and a broader idea as to the proper behavior during your next social interactions.

Finally, you might also want to consider whether there have been instances when you experienced the same issues. Patterns in your behavior could cause the same problems to arise, even if you're dealing with different people.

Taking a look back at previous encounters and trying to find trends can show you where you're most likely to fail during a social interaction. Some people might find that the problem lies in tactlessness, some find that the issue stems from their fixation on certain topics that a majority of individuals might find touchy or insulting.

Most of the time, these trends can be discovered with metacognition alone. However, there are some people who might need to experience confrontation once more to be able to accurately pinpoint where the problem exists. In this case, try to be mindful of what triggered the response during your interaction and make a mental note of the events as they occurred. This should make it easier to relieve the trend and adopt a healthier manner of interaction.

The Right Way to Behave

Imagine walking into a therapist's clinic for the first time. You've been invited to visit so that you can talk about childhood traumas, personal fears, problems, and other issues that might be eating up a part of your mental bandwidth. Needless to say, these are very personal, private concerns that you might not want to share, even with the closest people in your life.

So how do you think the therapist should act if she

wants to get the most honest information out of your meeting? If she had her arms crossed over her chest, if she chuckled when you shared particularly touchy information, if she winced at some of your stories, would you feel comfortable proceeding?

What if she were *too* accommodating? Asking a lot of questions? Overly reactive and empathizing with everything you said? Would she seem suspicious or pretentious? Would you feel comfortable continuing the session?

If there's anyone in present day that we can take cues from, it's therapists and counselors. Although their methods aren't entirely Holmesian, they do come pretty close. Their neutrality, their capability to ask the right questions at the right time, and their controlled reactions encourage people to share more truth without pretenses.

Given that, we can take away these basic aspects of the proper way to confront social interaction:

1. **Non-confrontational** - Have you ever noticed

how a therapist might continue to sit comfortably even when their client stands up, starts pacing, and acts agitated? It's a basic part of their profession to remain calm even in the face of an unsettled client.

Adapting a confrontational or aggressive demeanor can trigger one of two responses in your conversational partner and they look a lot like fight or flight. Those who have more confidence or who feel that they might have the opportunity to take the upper hand would match your aggression. Those who feel intimidated by your confrontational behavior would probably flee the situation.

Always make sure you're not displaying any signs of aggression, irritation, or anger. This helps mitigate arguments, even as the conversation becomes heated.

2. **Genuine** - How can you be pretentious when it comes to social interaction? Easy - act like you're *too interested or invested* in what's being communicated. While it is absolutely possible to

feel certain emotions especially when your conversational partner starts sharing touchy information, acting out of proportion might communicate that you're simply being theatrical.

To the person you're interacting with, the disproportionate display of emotion or reaction might be a poorly thought out strategy in order to get them to share more. The apparent lack of actual concern or care might be a turn off, which might actually cause them to hold back on how much they're willing to tell you.

How do you act *genuine* in the face of a new person? The answer isn't as complicated as it seems. Simply *be genuine*. Reacting based on how much emotion you actually feel will keep you from seeming uncaring or pretentious.

3. **Ask Only When Necessary** - If there's one thing about Sherlock that made him particularly efficient when collecting information was that he didn't interrupt anyone when they shared

details with him. He would stay silent, listen intently, and keep his thoughts and ideas to himself until the person was done sharing. In many cases, Sherlock wouldn't even ask any questions at all.

Holmes firmly believed that all the information you could ever need to properly dissect a situation (or a person) could be collected based off of what you're given. Asking questions was simply an *optional* part of the process mainly because of one thing - detachment.

Sherlock didn't involve his own prejudices, biases, or thoughts when he was being given information. He took the details as they were, so he rarely ever felt the need to ask a question. If ever he had to, it was only to clarify information that had already been given.

When dealing with a new person that you want to decode or decipher, try not to ask too many questions. Take what they say and pay attention to how they look - more often than not, you'll get everything you need out of just these two facets.

Asking questions tends to lead you down trains of thought that focus on your own egocentric tendencies, so it's often not recommended. If you find the need to ask a question, it's probably because you've allowed your thoughts or biases to interfere.

4. **Neutralize Body Language** - Later on in this guide, you'll learn just how much you can tell about a person based on body language and other non-verbal cues. These are potent markers that betray internal thoughts and feelings, allowing others to get a glimpse into a person's psyche by simply looking at how they're physically behaving.

In the same way that you can use these tools to understand the people around you, so too can others inspect your body language to learn more about you. Practicing how to neutralize your body language regardless of what might be going on in your mind can help make it a challenge for others to understand your true intentions, giving you the upper hand in any social interaction.

Generally, neutral body language starts with a neutral, relaxed posture. An open aura achieved through relaxed arms held at the side or with the hands gently clasped together can encourage another person to feel more comfortable. Leaning backward in a chair can also communicate a non-confrontational demeanor, creating a friendly atmosphere for your encounter.

Facial expressions too need to be carefully considered. Showing signs of your emotions can make a person adjust their behavior in order to mitigate any negativity they might cause you to experience. Keeping your face neutral and reacting minimally only when necessary can help maintain a natural interaction.

Honing Your Inner Holmes - DIY Experiment

Now that you've got some of the basics of behavior

down, it's time to polish them with a short test. This exercise is designed to help you understand your current social behavior so that you can get a better idea of what you need to change.

1. Find a quiet outdoor space where you might find a few strangers or passers-by. Try to find a place where you can sit comfortably and people watch.

2. Choose someone in the crowd at random. Observe their appearance, demeanor, and behavior. Once you have a well-established idea of who they might be, try to answer the following questions.

    A. How would you approach this person?

    B. How do you think this person would act given your approach?

    C. Do you think you'd get along with this person?

    D. What would you talk about to get them

interested in engaging with you?

3. Now, try to do some deep breathing exercises. Close your eyes, relax, and clear your mind of any thoughts that might interfere with your interactions. Take a few moments to breathe deliberately, feeling the air fill your lungs before letting out as much as you can.

4. Open your eyes and try to find the same person you observed earlier. This time, with your clear mind, try to answer the previous questions again.

5. Once you've finished answering the previous questions, try to audit your response with these guide questions.

   A. How did the breathing exercises help you become more aware of your behavior?

   B. Were there changes in the way you first answered the questions compared to the second attempt? What were they?

C. What tendencies or trends did you notice about your social behavior the first time you answered the questions? For instance, did you focus on a specific set of features? Were there any biases that you might have applied to your observations?

D. Given what you've learned, how do you think you can improve your approach so that you don't impart any influence on social interactions?

Chapter 3:

How to Control Your Own Behavior

"To comprehend yourself truly, which is also to comprehend the world truly, you needn't look any farther than at what abounds with life around you – the blossoming meadow, the untrodden woodlands. Without this as mankind's overriding objective, I don't foresee an age of actual enlightenment ever arriving."

- Sherlock Holmes, A Slight Trick of the Mind

Many times, Sherlock would find himself face to face with the perpetrator of the crime he would be investigating. And while the master detective likely had a sense of certainty in knowing that the person in front of him was responsible for the crime, he would maintain his silence and tell no one, even letting the criminal leave his presence without making an attempt to apprehend him.

But why?

Holmes knew that acting out and showing any signs of suspicion would tip the perpetrator and probably cause them to act in a way that would cover up his involvement. This change in behavior could easily cause confusion, and that's not something Sherlock wanted to deal with. He knew that the less guarded the perpetrator was, the more likely they would slip up and share information that could possibly incriminate him.

In the same way, showing the wrong behavior during an interaction could cause changes in the other person's behavior. This could make them act guarded, wary, and careful, and may even cause them to enact tactics that are intended to confuse you.

While we discussed the ideal behavior in the previous chapter, the way to achieve that kind of demeanor isn't quite as obvious. How can you control yourself so that you don't end up altering the behavior of people around you?

Controlling Your Own Behavior

Watson would often describe Sherlock as being full of himself, and he would question whether the master detective even felt human emotion on the typical scale that most of us do. If anything, Holmes was an arrogant man and he *knew* for a fact that he was more intellectually capable than most others around him.

Despite that though, he was able to hold back his tendencies and keep his opinions to himself. He was exceptionally talented at maintaining neutrality and keeping his mouth shut even if he probably always knew better than those around him. How did he manage to do that given that he did have an arrogant nature to him?

The answer is simple. Sherlock had taught himself *how* to control his behavior. Knowing his tendencies made it easier to apply the necessary changes, and thus get a hold of his impulses before they ruined the moment and gave his thoughts away.

Deep Breathing Exercises

Notice how when you're just about to explode with emotions, your breathing starts to race. This natural reaction is your body's way of coping with an increased blood pressure and heart rate, which both happen when you're brewing with heightened emotions.

Breathing deliberately, slowly, deeply, and from the stomach can help calm the nervous system and clear the mind. This can keep you from acting on impulse, allowing you to exercise greater control over your emotions, your thoughts, and your actions.

In many instances, Holmes would be described closing his eyes and breathing slowly and deliberately while he was being given information at a crime scene. This helped him keep his thoughts in check and prevent himself from saying anything that could interfere with the other person's behavior.

So, how can you perform deep breathing exercises properly to achieve the ideal socialization behavior? More importantly, how can you perform deep breathing in front of another person without giving yourself away?

1. **Unclench** - When confronted with another person who's talking or acting in a way that you might not find appealing or agreeable, the tendency is to clench the body.

Your shoulders might stiffen, you might feel your fists clenched tightly, and you might start to grind your teeth. These are all normal reactions when trying to control your impulses. But it can show outsiders that you're currently under stress.

Unclenching your body can help make deep breathing far more effective. This can be done by simply *letting go*. Start by sensing your face and detecting if your expression is tense. Relax your brows and try to keep your lips neutral. Then, move down to your shoulders. If they're raised and stiff, slowly let them go and drop them to their neutral position. Do this until you reach your feet, unclenching areas as you go along.

2. **Mindset** - Having the proper mentality can significantly improve the outcomes of deep breathing. For instance, if you refuse to let go of negative thoughts or prejudices when you engage in deep breathing, then you might end up reinforcing these thoughts during the process. So instead of adapting the proper behavior, you would end up justifying and rationalizing your biases and tendencies.

With each full inhale, try to release your thoughts. The most difficult to deal with would be your own emotions, especially because most of us have been conditioned to operate on what we feel. Unfortunately, running on emotions can be very detrimental to social interactions.

As you exhale, let go of assumptions, biases, and

233

ideas that could possibly interfere with the way you perceive or interact with other people.

3. **Breathe From the Stomach** - Deep breathing is actually synonymous with belly breathing - a unique breathing pattern that encourages you to inflate the abdomen instead of the chest. This form of breathing is particularly calming, known to help reduce heart rate and normalize blood pressure.

When trying to perform deep breathing, be sure to breathe into your abdomen. Take each breath slowly and try to feel the air as it fills your lungs. Hold each breath for around 3 seconds before completely releasing the air and inhaling again.

Empathize

We see the world through our own self-tinted glasses. What does that mean? It simply means that anything and everything around us is often interpreted according to how we think these different things might benefit or affect us. For instance, a teenage daughter being reprimanded by her mother for coming home late might think that her mother is being controlling and unreasonable, unable to see the reason why her parent might be acting that way.

Empathizing with someone - even if you've only just met - can help neutralize any feelings you might have. Take this scenario for example.

You're sitting in a cafe, enjoying a cup of coffee while you read your favorite book, and a woman comes barging in. She's shouting at the top of her lungs, looking for the owner of a vehicle she described to look just like your own. You slowly raise your hand and say that it sounds like she's talking about your car, and then she rushes to the side of your table and starts throwing minor insults your way.

How do you respond?

Considering that you've just met this woman, it's likely that you might find yourself wanting to engage in argument. *How dare she talk to me like this - it's mortifying!* Of course, the situation might cause a few heads to turn in your direction, but there are better ways to deal with this woman.

Firstly, you might want to take a few deep breaths. Before you address her, observe her behavior and her appearance. What could be her reason for acting this way? Would a normal person lash out at a stranger for no apparent reason? Probably not. What does she want you to do and what is she communicating to you?

As it turns out, your car was in the way of her vehicle, making it impossible for her to back up and drive away. She stopped by the coffee shop to pick up a drink for her boss who had no patience for late arrivals. This made her feel agitated, knowing how it might affect her work.

Putting everything into perspective, it's easy to see that while her reaction might not have been the best or the most appropriate, it definitely wasn't without reason. Learning to empathize with others in this way can help you control your emotions, especially when you come to realize that you might act similarly had you been put in a similar situation.

Add Context

Did you know that people are inclined to behave differently and put on a charade when faced with a potential employer? Did you know that people tend to wear different 'masks' depending on where they might be and who they might be communicating with?

We as a human race have evolved to *fake* interactions, especially when we feel that our typical behavior might not be ideal for a specific situation. Understanding this should help you become more receptive of other people and the way they might act around you.

We're often urged to adjust ourselves when the people around us don't act how we anticipate them to. *Why is this person avoiding eye contact? I should probably try to look more amicable. Why are they too close? I should square off my shoulders and lean away. Why do they seem aggressive? I should cross my arms and show them that I'm not intimidated.*

Don't. Remember that there is a context to every situation, and these people are probably showing you behavior based on *how* they think they should approach this particular interaction. Remain neutral and don't let them sway you into acting a certain kind of way.

Keep the Goal in Mind

One of the best ways to remember to keep your cool and to avoid tainting the interaction would be to keep your goal in mind. Your objective to decode and understand a person at a glance should be paramount to any emotional response that they might inspire.

In many cases, other people can make you feel upset or even angry simply by stating their own thoughts and opinions. Of course, it can be particularly difficult to resist the urge to fight back and respond how you would like to, but there are greater returns to taking the time to *understand* their behavior first.

By allowing yourself the cool, calm, collectedness that it takes to be able to properly decode a person first, you can stay one step ahead and react in the best possible way to avoid confrontation and arguments.

The Theory of Masks

An important aspect of understanding people at a glance involves understanding how each person has a tendency to use a mask. Even in their own personal space, a person might don a specific mask which makes it difficult to understand the true self.

Depending on the situation, it's possible that a person might use one of a variety of masks, allowing them to assume the most ideal self during a specific encounter. So how a person acts around family might be different from how they might act around coworkers.

Some people might develop masks to cover up specific traumas that they might have had in their earlier years. Those who suffered through abusive relationships as children have very intricate masks that make them exceptionally effective at deflecting any other people's efforts to get a glance into their truth.

These masks often work as defense mechanisms because humans are generally protective of their true self. Our objective during social interactions is to make sure that we're putting our best foot forward. No one wants other people to see the ugly realities of their actual selves, which is why it has become instinctual for us to wear masks to please the others around us.

What's tricky about masks is that they can be changed at a moment's notice. Most people can adapt and adjust their social mask in order to respond to slight cues in their given social engagement. For instance, a woman who feels that her date might think she's boring will adjust her posture and start talking about some of the more exciting events in her life, deflecting that train of thought and making him feel otherwise.

That said, it's important that you consider the theory of masks when trying to decode others around you. Using neutrality when dealing with a target will help keep them from adding layers to their mask, making it possible for you to see closer to the truth. The more encounters you have with someone, the less guarded they will become. So over time, that mask can change.

Honing Your Inner Holmes - DIY Experiment

Using the tips provided in this chapter and the previous one, try to respond to the following situations. Choose the answers that best suit your reactions in the options provided and see how well your choices match the ideal responses.

Scenario 1

A friend has set you up on a blind date with a someone who is a stranger to you. All you know about them is that they work at the local museum while completing their last few years of college.

You meet up at a local restaurant for dinner and they greet you with a timid handshake. After asking a few routine questions, the air turns silent and your date starts fiddling with their fork. They glance away and look at neighboring tables, giggling nervously as they point out something irrelevant in an attempt to clear the air of silence.

What do you do?

A. Prompt them with a question to start a conversation.

B. Let the air of awkwardness continue.

C. Ask them if they want to change the venue.

Scenario 2

At your work desk, you find a sticky note plastered across your computer screen. "See me IMMEDIATELY!" it says, scribbled in your boss' penmanship. You just got back from lunch and visited your desk to grab your toothbrush, so you dash quickly to the restroom and freshen up before seeing your superior.

You knock on his door and peer inside. You see him sitting at his desk with his hands on his head and his elbows resting on the table - a look of frustration drawn across his face. "What IS this?" he asks you. He's referring to a report that you submitted a few weeks ago.

The document was a summary of projections

expected for the next few months of operations. The numbers weren't to his liking, but they were as accurate as you could manage. After all, the purpose of the report was to forecast the upcoming months, not to sugarcoat how things might happen.

He tells you to redo the entire report, which took you about a month to finalize. And on top of that, he requires that you render mandatory overtime so that you have time to work on the new output. Unfortunately for you, you've already made plans with your partner to spend time together since the past few months have been exceptionally busy for both of you.

How do you respond to your boss?

A. Apologize and say that you can't render mandatory overtime because you have prescheduled engagements.

B. Agree to his conditions and apologize for the way the initial report came out.

C. Offer to give an in-depth explanation of the

report.

Answers

We all respond differently based on our own character and personality, but knowing how Sherlock does it should make it easier to react to social situations as ideally as possible.

Scenario 1

In the first scenario, your date is showing obvious signs of shyness. The routine questions, the aversion to eye contact, and the psychomotor activity in the form of fiddling with a fork are all classic signals that manifest a timid personality or uncertainty in that specific situation.

While it was explained that asking questions is an optional route when trying to decode a new person, you need to place this meeting in its context. A date requires more interaction, so it's important to make sure that you contribute to the engagement.

Given that, it's ideal that you add to the conversation *without* altering her behavior. This means that you should try to avoid conversation starters that *suggest* that she share a specific pre-determined answer. This simply means that you should prompt her with a question (Option A) without giving her a hint as to what answer you're hoping to hear.

For instance, some questions are laced with hints that direct the individual towards an 'ideal' answer. "I'm a big supporter of animal welfare. How do you feel about animals?" With the initial statement, you've already told your date that you *like* animals, and of course, it would possibly be ideal for you that your date likes them, too.

Anyone in that situation would probably provide an answer that would impress the person asking, because the goal of a date would be to win the other person over. So even if they weren't particularly interested in animals, they might come up with some exaggeration of the truth or perhaps even a complete lie just to leave a good impression.

The best questions are open ended and non-suggestive, allowing the other individual to come up with an honest answer that could lead to further communication.

Scenario 2

In the second scenario, it's easy to see that your boss was upset about the numbers that came up in your report. Obviously, this wasn't the result of your mistakes, but the result of the actual data made available to you for the document. That said, it would be difficult to come to different results even if you repeated the entire process, given that you didn't commit any mistakes in the first.

Putting yourself in his shoes, it's apparent that his anger was possibly stemming from distress. The projections were less than ideal, and he was probably taking his anger out on the nearest possible target - you. Seeing things from his perspective, it's easier to see why he might be acting the way that he is.

It's always tricky dealing with a superior because of the power they have over us. In this case, your boss can have a direct impact on your job and career, so making the wrong move could result to detrimental outcomes for your work life.

In this case, the best option would be to explain your report (option C) to give your boss a better understanding of the numbers that appear in your document. Responding in a quiet, calm, and apologetic yet professional tone can help appease your boss and give you the opportunity to clarify the results of your calculations.

Chapter 4:

How To Interpret Personality Types

"London, noisy, noisome, nattering London: aged, ageless, dignified, eccentric in her ways - seat of empire, capital of all the world; that indomitable grey lady of drab aspect but sparkling personality - was at her very, very best and most radiant. And Holmes, ebullient and uncommonly chatty, was in a mood to match."

Let's hop back into the previous chapter and take a closer look at the second scenario in the DIY experiment. Given this reaction, what kind of personality do you think your boss had? Do you think he would have acted differently if he had a different personality? Yes, he probably would have. But *why* would a difference in personality have made a change in reaction?

An individual's 'personality' is loosely defined as a

collection of traits and characteristics that give people their distinctive character. Throughout the years, there have been *countless* psychologists who have tried to encapsulate the meaning of a personality - from Freud, to Erikson, to Jung, and many others - and all of these experts have contributed greatly to our understanding of the abstract concept.

Essentially, our personality tells us what we think are the acceptable, ideal, and appropriate social reactions. Our inhibitions are dictated by our personalities, so there are some things that we may or may not do depending on our specific combination of unique characteristics. That's why some people find it easy to engage in arguments, while others find it more practical and reasonable to avoid confrontation even when they have all the reason to be upset.

Knowing an individual's personality is an important part of decoding people because it tells you *how* they might act or speak. Their personality will show you their tendencies and social patterns, allowing you to generate a more accurate prediction of how a specific encounter might go.

The Myers Briggs Test

Carl Jung was a Swiss psychiatrist and psychoanalyst who dedicated most of his life to understanding the human psyche. Through his research, he was able to publish several books that gave readers his interpretations and understanding of the human personality. Soon, English translations of these books found their way into the hands of Katharine Cook Briggs - an academic and an avid reader and writer.

Prior to finding Jung's books, Briggs had already developed her own theories on personality. She formulated 4 categories of personality types after noticing that her soon-to-be son-in-law had a different set of characteristics compared to members of their family. Upon reading Jung's books however, she discovered that the psychoanalyst had a far more extensive understanding of personality.

This prompted her to further develop her system, which led to the iconic Myers-Briggs Type Indicator - a personality test that she developed with her daughter, Isabel Briggs Myers. This test is now used widely in employment and school evaluations.

Limitations of the Myers-Briggs Type Indicator

While it is widely used and applied in various fields of practice, the Myers-Briggs Type Indicator isn't without its flaws. In fact, throughout the years, countless critics have made comments about the MBTI's reliability, especially because it can give a person different results with each take.

On top of that, the test does not take neuroticism into account. So individuals with neurotic tendencies might not be detected by the exam.

Finally, the test doesn't provide any accurate measures for what it detects, so it's hard to understand exactly *what* it tries to understand given that the concept of personality is so abstract.

Even then, using the Myers-Briggs for purposes that include decoding a person can be good enough to get a better understanding of what lies underneath the surface. However, as any cautious detective, you need to be aware of the method's limitations to guide your premises and conclusions.

Concepts and Basics

The Myers-Briggs Type Indicator (or MBTI) is a personality test that can result to 1 of 16 different personalities. The test is administered by asking the examinee to indicate whether they agree or disagree to a statement by choosing an answer from a scale. This also measures the extent to which they agree or disagree.

Each personality type is defined by an acronym of 4 letters, each one corresponding to the specific inclination or tendency a person has which is determined to be *most prominent* in a list of dichotomies. There are 3 subcategories, and these are *attitudes, functions,* and *lifestyle preferences*.

Attitudes

The first letter in every Myers-Briggs personality type refers to either extroversion or introversion so that each of the 16 types will either appear EXXX or IXXX. This first letter designates the individual's attitude, which was described by Myers as the tendency to act either inwardly or outwardly on thoughts and ideas.

Essentially, extroverts are more inclined to *execute action*. They move and speak to fuel their motivation. Without this physical manifestation of energy, their motivation has a tendency to decline. People who are introverts are more likely to reflect and think. They prefer inward manifestations of their energy, and are more motivated with tasks that require rumination and deep thought.

Here are some of the basic differences of introverts and extroverts:

Extroverts	Introverts
Action oriented	Thought oriented
Prefer a wide knowledge base that crosses over to different concepts	Prefer a deep knowledge base that explains specific information in detail
Enjoy frequent interaction	Enjoy meaningful interaction
Draw energy from socialization	Draw energy from being alone

How do you identify an extrovert or introvert in public? Of course, drawing this information back to Sherlock, the true value of knowing the attitude types is being able to detect them in real life situations. In this case, you might consider someone an extrovert if they seem to enjoy socializing, if they seem energized with physical activity, and if they present a commanding aura that takes control of interactions.

You might call someone an introvert if they prefer isolation, if they enjoy small meaningful gatherings and socialization, or if they seem energized when given the opportunity to explore ideas, thoughts, and concepts away from the company of other people.

During social interactions, it's possible that someone who is an extrovert might be more interested in direct engagement and conversation. They also tend to be far more vocal about their ideas and opinions, making them quite the challenge to debate with. On the other hand, someone who is an introvert might be much more comfortable having you take the reins of a conversation.

Introverts, as a general rule, are far harder to

decode because they internalize everything they think and feel. However, because they are more interested in *meaningful* interaction, tapping into what they find important and relevant can make it possible for you to get them to become more expressive.

Functions

There are two pairs of functions according to Myers - these are the perceiving and the judging functions. The **perceiving** functions describe how a person interprets information or data, and the **judging** functions indicate a person's tendencies when it comes to making a decision based on the facts that have been presented.

The perceiving functions are **sensation** and **intuition**. As a general rule, people have *dominant* traits in a specific dichotomy, but it never means that the other is completely disabled. Everyone has these traits to some extent, it's just that one or the other is more prominent and likely to be used.

Sensation pertains to a method of information processing that uses the 5 senses. This is a more empirical method of data interpretation in which a person prefers to rely on details that are perceivable. They prefer to dwell on data that's present, tangible, and *real* as opposed to information that comes from hunches or guesswork.

Intuition on the other hand, is a method of information processing that dwells more on the unseen. These people use their gut to feel for the right conclusion, even if that means their conclusion won't be based on factual, tangible information. They're often more interested in the possibilities of the future, so they won't limit themselves to choices that are bound by facts.

The judging functions are **thinking** and **feeling**. These are decision making functions that are used when a person needs to arrive at a resolve given a set of information.

258

As the term suggests, people who use their **thinking function** to make a decision choose to do so from a somewhat detached standpoint. They use logic and reason, and prefer to look at the facts before arriving at a thoroughly thought-out decision. However that decision affects their emotions or the emotions of others around them isn't a top concern in the decision making process.

On the other hand, people who use their **feeling function** when making a decision are more inclined to use the emotional context of the situation instead of simply dwelling on the facts. They prefer outcomes that generate harmony, making choices that suit the benefit and preference of the general census.

According to Jung, each person uses a dominant function in combination with an auxiliary function. The psychoanalyst has also suggested that we use a tertiary function to a much lesser extent, with the fourth function taking the role of a 'shadow'. In all cases, the shadow or fourth function is the opposite of the dominant function.

Lifestyle Preferences

In this dichotomy, there are two options - **judging** and **perception**. This is an added facet of the Myers-Briggs Type Indicator which wasn't available in Carl Jung's model. The purpose of this dichotomy is to decipher a person's preference in using either their judging or perceiving functions.

People who manifest the judging function as their lifestyle preference are those who navigate the world using their judging function most predominantly. This means that TJ individuals (or *thinking/judging*) are seen as logical people, while FJ individuals (or *feeling/judging*) are seen as empathetic.

In the same way, people who tend to prefer the perception navigate the world using one of the two perceiving functions. That said, individuals who are

SP (*sensation/perceiving*) are seen as concrete individuals who use reliable facts. Those who are NP (*intuitive/perceiving*) are usually considered or labeled abstract thinkers.

The 16 Personality Types

Although Jung had originally come up with 32 personality types, the Myers-Briggs Type Indicator condensed the types into just 16. These personality types use combinations in each dichotomy to come up with a holistic idea of a person's *tendencies*.

While it doesn't specifically predict a person's reactions, it does tell you the kind of response you can expect. The personality types shed light on the type of interaction a particular person might prefer, given the specifics they fall into under each dichotomy.

ISTJ	ISFJ	INFJ	INTJ
Sincere, analytical, reserved, realistic, hardworking, responsible, and trustworthy	Warm, considerate, gentle, thorough, pragmatic, devoted, caring, helpful, responsible	Idealistic, organized, compassionate, gentle, prefer harmony, enjoy intellectual stimulation	Original, innovative, independent, strategic, logical, reserved, insightful, driven
ISTP	ISFP	INFP	INTP
Action-oriented, enjoy understanding the mechanical functions	Gentle, sensitive, flexible, helpful, realistic, interested in	Sensitive, creative, idealistic, caring, puts great value on inner harmony	Logical, precise, reserved, flexible, original, enjoy speculatio

of things, spontaneo us, analytical	practicali ty, strive for a personal space that's logical and beautiful	and peace, focuses on dreams and goals	n, can come up with creative solutions to problems, imaginativ e
ESTP Outgoing, realistic, action-oriented, curious, pragmatic, skilled negotiator	ESFP Playful, skilled at negotiati ng, strong common sense, friendly, spontane ous,	ENFP Enthusiastic , creative, spontaneou s, optimistic, supportive, enjoys engaging in new projects	ENTP Inventive, enthusiast ic, versatile, inquisitive , strategic, enterprisi ng, enjoys new and unfamiliar

	tactful		challenges
ESTJ	ESFJ	ENFJ	ENTJ
Efficient, outgoing, analytical, realistic, systematic, dependable	Friendly, outgoing, reliable, practical, helpful, prefer to please others, enjoys activity and productivity	Caring, enthusiastic, idealistic, organized, diplomatic, responsible, skilled communicators	Strategic, logical, efficient, outgoing, ambitious, long range planners, effective at organizing people

Understanding the personality types entails breaking its corresponding acronym down into parts. The first letter always represents the **attitude** which would either be extroverted or introverted.

The second and third letters are representative of the **functions**. As a general rule, this letter combination *can't* be represented by two letters from the same dichotomy. For instance, an individual can't be both *sensing* and *intuitive* since they're both perceiving functions. A person can't be both *thinking* and *feeling* since they're both judging functions. That said, the only combinations for the second and third letters can be **SF, ST, NF,** or **NT.**

Finally, the last letter in the 4 letter acronym represents the lifestyle preference for that specific personality. This can be either *perceiving* represented by P or *judging* represented by J.

All that considered, we can now decipher that a person who falls within the ISFJ personality type - the most common among the population - manifests an *introvert-sensing-feeling-judging* personality type.

Keep in mind that there's far more to each of these

personality types than what's stated in this short table. In fact, each type comes with extensive elaborations that discuss the personality in depth, so it might be worth reading up on the different types to familiarize yourself with each one.

Stocking points of information for each type into your mind palace can help give you keys to understanding each person you encounter based on the type that you identify them to be.

Detecting Personality Types in Real Life

Is there any way that you can accurately determine a person's personality type based on the Myers-Briggs Type Indicator *without* putting them through the entire test process? The answer is **no**, you can't. Some of the factors in the Myers-Briggs personality types can only be determined by asking specific questions, so it might be impossible to get an accurate representation by strict observation.

On top of that, people have a tendency to wear a 'mask' depending on who they're in front of or where they are. Remember that according to Myers, just because a specific function is dominant, doesn't mean the others are disabled. For instance, a thinking person still has the capacity to feel, and a sensing person still has the capacity for intuition.

That said, some people will rely on less dominant functions if they feel that their current situation calls for it. For example, a person who doesn't like their job might use a secondary or even a tertiary function in order to finish the tasks at hand.

With that in mind, it's advisable that you avoid jumping to conclusions when trying to detect a person's personality type. Of course, Sherlock was able to decode personalities much faster, but we have to consider our own limitations as well as the possible 'masks' that people might wear to throw us off and improve their public image.

So, how can you accurately interpret an individual's personality type in the real world *without* putting them through the test? It's going to be tricky, but it is possible.

Are They Quick to Respond?

When interacting with someone, consider the speed at which they choose to answer questions. Do they respond almost instantaneously, providing long, drawn out answers that make it seem like they had these answers ready? Do they sound like they're thinking out loud, perhaps even dwelling into other topics from the actual answer to your question?

Or do they take their time before giving a response? Do they think about their answer before handing it over, and are their answers more limited and concise?

So, what's the relevance of being able to answer immediately or otherwise? Well, taking a closer look at this interaction behavior tells you whether a person is an introvert or an extrovert - the first letter in the personality acronym.

Generally speaking, extroverts are far more inclined to answer questions as if they're dictating what they're thinking because that's how they *think*. They function more efficiently in social interactions when they can voice out what they have to say, which substantially improves their train of thought. They NEED to think out loud because it's how they're able to come up with the best ideas.

On the other hand, introverts are the exact opposite. They prefer internalizing their thoughts, which is why they might take their time to ruminate before answering a question. They're less energized by social interaction and work best when they're left to their own devices, and it shows when you consider how they prefer to answer questions.

Conversations with introverts tend to be more laid back, logical, and slow paced, giving each contributor the opportunity to deliberate their answers and enjoy enough white space in order to craft a thorough response. On the other side of the spectrum, someone who's an extrovert might not give you the light of day.

These people *love* having the opportunity to talk which often takes over certain social graces. This means they might end up overpowering others involved, preventing them from sharing their own thoughts. In the event that two extroverts end up in conversation, then you might find them talking over each other in a conversational mess that almost sounds like unintelligible rambling.

Do They Like Talking About the Present or Past, or the Future?

You'll notice how some people seem to be far more interested in talking about things that have already happened or things that are currently happening, as opposed to things that *might* happen. These people obviously like to dwell on facts, and find it more reasonable to discuss things that are tangible and real.

In the same way, there are some people who prefer

talking about things that could happen in the future. The thought of possibilities and the excitement of exploring what *might be* can be particularly interesting for these types of people, and they enjoy dwelling on ideas that aren't yet guaranteed or proven, but are likely to be true in the future.

If the person you're trying to decode is showcasing an interest in the tangible, or the things that have already happened, then they're likely to prefer their *sensing* function. If they prefer discussing the future possibilities, then they're likely inclined to use their *intuitive* function.

Do They Consider How Others are Affected?

People who use their *feeling* function are often more inclined to think about the way their decisions affect others around them. They're not always after the *best outcomes*, but are rather more interested in the *best solution for the people involved*.

On the other hand, the *thinking* individual makes decisions based on logical reason. How that choice affects others isn't exactly a major consideration when it comes to deciding on the best solution, as long as they arrive at the optimal outcomes given the specific problem.

Take this scenario for example: three families are on a road trip that's scheduled to run for about 8 hours. Each family will ride their own car, and the 2 cars will follow the head of the convoy to lead the way.

Two cars are both SUVs, capable of driving over rough terrain, which opens up the possibility of taking shortcuts that could reduce travel time to just 6 hours. This would be beneficial as it would prevent the risk of paying a late fee at the hotel, since they might arrive after the designated check-in hours if they travel the entire 8 hour stretch.

Unfortunately however, the third family is driving a sedan that can't tread through the dangerous, off-road terrain on the designated shortcut. So now, the families have to decide:

A. Two SUVs will travel through the shortcut and provide the sedan instructions on the long route in order to reach the hotel in time and avoid the late fee.

B. All three vehicles will travel the long route and just split the late fee among the three families when they arrive at their accommodations.

A *feeling* person would likely choose the second option because it *benefits everyone involved*. They would take everyone's emotional welfare into consideration, and use that to weigh heavily on an answer to a problem.

A *thinking* person would likely choose the first option because it comes up with the logical result. No one wants to pay a late fee, and given the proper directions, it's unlikely that the family in the sedan would be lost. Of course, that doesn't take the feelings of the third family into account, but the outcomes are optimal if they want to save money and time.

How can you determine if a person is *thinking* or *feeling?* Easy - asking questions about real life, world events can help showcase the logic they use to justify the decisions made by others around them. For instance, you can ask them about political events and then pay attention to find out whether they're inclined to choose what's *practical* or what's *empathetic.*

Are They Flexible or Rigid?

Imagine this scenario: Karen and Jonah are just about ready to have dinner. They had planned to cook up an elaborate meal to celebrate a recent promotion. However, since it has been a rather stressful day, Karen asks Jonah whether he'd like to have dinner out instead.

"Dinner out? But we already planned this dinner. Let's just reschedule your suggestion for tomorrow night." To which Karen responded, "Okay, do you want to try the new seafood place or do you want to make reservations at our usual?"

"The new seafood place sounds good," Jonah replies. The next day comes and just as night starts to fall, they're both getting ready to leave. "You know," Karen says, "there's this other restaurant we haven't tried. Marge told me they have the best tacos."

"We already decided on the new seafood place yesterday!" Jonah exclaims. "Let's not make any changes and just get our plan done."

Are you a Jonah or a Karen? If you consider yourself flexible and adaptable (like Karen), then you're likely a *perceiving* person. These people know that life isn't always as we plan, and so they revel in the ever changing flux of things around them. They're spontaneous and ready for everything, and they don't necessarily need plans to have a good time.

If you're more like Jonah, then that means you might be a *judging* person. These people like structure and certainty, and might feel thrown off if they don't get to follow their designated pattern of events. On the upside however, they are exceptionally talented at coming up with surefire plans and executing them, making them intelligent and efficient leaders.

Now What?

So, how do you use this understanding of personalities to be able to decode people at a glance? Remember that Myers specifically indicated that her Type Indicator wasn't a predictive measure to tell how people act or to measure their socialization preferences. Rather, it's an indicator of *tendencies*. Everyone has the *tendency* to act in more ways than one, but this Type Indicator allows us to see which tendency is dominant.

Understanding where a person falls under the 16 different personality types will shed light on their behavior and will thus give you a more reliable basis on which to establish how you should respond to them.

Honing Your Inner Holmes - DIY Experiment

Here's a fun test that you can try for yourself or that you might want to try on other people. These questions - although seemingly unrelated and irrelevant - are designed to give you a better idea of your own personality type. You can also use it to try to decode other peoples' personality types as well, according to the Myers-Briggs Type Indicator.

1. I like to...

    A. Meet new people and engage in social activities

B. Stay at home and indulge in my favorite books and movies

2. I rely more on...

   A. Tangible facts and proven truths

   B. Abstract thoughts and future possibilities

3. I base my decisions off of...

   A. Logic, reason, and rational thought to arrive at the best outcomes

   B. Empathy and the way the decision works for the general census

4. I prefer to...

   A. Have matters settled and be done with it

   B. Keep my options open for greater spontaneity

If you answered:

1. A - Extrovert

B - Introvert

2. A - Sensing

   B - Intuition

3. A - Thinking

   B - Feeling

4. A - Judging

   B - Perceiving

Chapter 5:

Holmes' Super Power - The Art Of Induction

"So what is the truth?" Mr. Umezaki had once asked him. "How do you arrive at it? How do you unravel the meaning of something that doesn't want to be known?"

- Mr. Umezaki, A Slight Trick of the Mind

Often, we mistake inductive reasoning for deductive reasoning because we hear the term *deductive* reasoning more commonly in the media! In fact, even Arthur Conan Doyle himself mistook one for the other, thinking that his character was a master of deduction when he was, in fact, a master of *induction*.

What makes them different?

To put it plainly, *deductive* reasoning is the process of logical reasoning that entails *taking* or *deducing* information from pre-established fact. Take this train of thought for example:

A. The authorities claim that this person was murdered. (FACT)

B. A bloodied knife is present in the room (OBSERVATION)

C. Thus, this bloodied knife must be the murder weapon (CONCLUSION)

It is *known* that the victim was murdered, and this becomes the basis for interpreting all the other information in the room. Thus, any observations made at the scene of the crime will be tied back to the initial fact.

On the other hand, consider this train of thought:

A. You walk into a room and find a dead body (OBSERVATION)

B. Near the body is a bloody knife (OBSERVATION)

C. There are stab wounds on the body (OBSERVATION)

D. The victim's hands are tied behind his back (OBSERVATION)

E. It would have been improbable for this person to stab himself given that his hands were bound (INFERENCE)

F. It's likely that someone else did this to this person (INFERENCE)

G. This person was murdered (CONCLUSION)

Upon entering this crime scene, you don't know any of the details. So any evidence that you collect at the scene will be treated as an observation. After collecting enough evidence, you can come up with inferences, or ideas as to how this information ties together. By considering the possibilities given the situation, you can then come up with a conclusion.

Often, Sherlock would wow the police and Watson with his superior inductive logic, which was often misbranded as deductive reasoning. The master detective had a knack for taking bits of information and details from each person he would encounter to be able to formulate a general idea or conclusion as to who they were, where they've been, what work they do, and many other extrapolations.

Using Inductive Reasoning to Decode Others

When Holmes and Watson first met, they knew close to nothing about each other, aside from the fact that they would now share lodging. Sherlock had to look for someone to split rent with him since he had been running short on funds. And that's how their paths crossed.

As they were introduced to one another, Sherlock said "You've been in Afghanistan, I perceive." He wasn't asking Watson for a confirmation, but was rather stating a fact. This surprised the good doctor. Sherlock didn't explain how he came to discover that bit of information until later on in the book, when John Watson tells him that he believes someone had told Sherlock of his recent trip to Afghanistan.

Sherlock explains no, that no one had told him and that he instead pieced together information based on what he saw and drew his conclusion from there.

Here's what Holmes' train of thought might have looked like upon their first meeting:

A. Watson's face and hands are a darker tone from the skin under his cuff and collar.

B. This could mean that he was in a place that exposed him to harsh sunlight. Possibly a vacation?

C. If he were on vacation, then his entire body would have been tan.

D. He was not on vacation.

E. He was probably in a tropical country performing work-related activities under the sun.

F. Watson mentioned attending Bart's - a popular training ground for doctors.

G. Watson must be a doctor.

H. His stance is stiff and rigid, what someone might consider the typical stance of someone serving in the military.

I. John is likely an army doctor.

J. His arm is held in an awkward manner, as though it causes him pain.

K. It might have been injured.

L. Considering all the premises, it can be concluded that John was an army doctor serving in a tropical country.

M. The Anglo-Afghan war concluded just last year. It was in Afghanistan.

N. John was an army doctor serving in Afghanistan, and was medically discharged after an injury.

Well, that was quite the mental exercise wasn't it? Sherlock had nothing more to go on than the things that Watson said during their first meeting, and the good doctor's general appearance. Piecing together all of this information without any pre-established facts, Holmes used his *inductive* reasoning to arrive at an accurate conclusion.

While it might take some getting used to, becoming adept at the use of inductive reasoning is very possible. Familiarizing yourself with the process and understanding the cornerstones of this unique type of logic can make it much easier to use it in real, practical situations.

Keep Your Eyes and Ears Sharp

Just like Sherlock, it's vital that you keep your senses sharp if you want to make the most of inductive logic. A lot of information can easily fly over your head if you're not paying attention, putting gaps in your premises and making it hard to piece things together.

Many of the little details you'll have to collect will be considered irrelevant and unnecessary by most, and at the start, you yourself might think that some information seems unimportant. But developing a keen eye that picks up on even the most minute details can help you collate enough information to come to the most accurate conclusion.

Observe as much of the person as possible, scan their body, grooming, their clothes, and mannerisms. Avoid putting labels or meanings on these readings unless you've weighed all the possibilities, and then decided on the most rational and realistic premise.

Leverage Online Tests

There are numerous websites that offer tests to measure and challenge your inductive reasoning skills. Tests are usually focused on finding patterns, and require you to find the missing or the next shape in a sequence.

These tests can be taken for free and are incredibly effective at sharpening your inductive reasoning skills. There are also a variety of other test formats that provide you situational questions, allowing you to flex your inductive reasoning muscle to piece the picture together.

Practice on Real People

Most of the people we see or come across during the day will probably always be strangers to us, so there really won't be a way to verify if the conclusions you arrive at through inductive logic would be true or not. But it doesn't hurt to practice your skill when you can.

Taking the time to try to figure out more about the people you see in your day to day life can be particularly effective at helping you hone your inductive reasoning logic. This should train your eye to be far more sensitive when picking up minute details, and may even help you establish contexts for specific features that you would commonly observe.

Honing Your Inner Holmes - DIY Experiment

Here's a test to exercise your inductive reasoning. The next time you find yourself in a social interaction with a new person, try to use this short guide to help you learn more about them.

Keep in mind that while it is possible to use inductive reasoning to learn more about old friends, we tend to have biases when it comes to people we already know. So when sharpening your inductive logic, always try to find someone new.

- ☐ Observe the person's *fluid* traits. These are qualities that are not fixed and can be changed depending on preference or situation. (i.e. Hair, clothing, grooming, etc.)

☐ How are they kept? Are they well-maintained? Do you notice wear? Are they worn out and faded? Does it seem to be changed/cleaned/worn frequently?

☐ Based on what you've observed concerning fluid traits, what can you surmise regarding this individual's personality? Are they careful, meticulous, polished? Or do they seem carefree, free-spirited, and spontaneous? What other personality traits can you assume?

Observing the non-fluid features on your target can shed light on a variety of details, some of which might not be as obvious to the typical observer. For instance, wear markings on a boot or a watch strap could indicate that that particular item is used frequently.

In some cases, it could also indicate routine. For

instance, wear over an area of a watch strap could be because that person frequently fidgets with that part. The trick is trying to put context to the person's entire being by piecing together the different factors that they present. The more you're able to put together, the easier it becomes to put context into each specific detail.

Chapter 6:

The Body Scan Method

"Your problem, dear chap, as I have had occasion to remind you, is that you see but you do not observe; you hear but you do not listen. For a literary man, Watson - and note that I do not comment on the merit of your latest account of my little problems - for a man with the pretenses of being a writer, you are singularly unobservant. Honestly, sometimes I am close to despair."

- Sherlock Holmes, The Whitechapel Horrors

When Holmes told Watson that he perceived the doctor had come from Afghanistan, Watson's surprise was two-fold - one, because he knew for a fact that he hadn't told anyone that he had come from Afghanistan. And two, because he couldn't quite figure out how Sherlock would have figure it out. After all, they had just met.

Sherlock had a knack for keeping his methods concealed. So even as he scanned Watson's entire physique, the doctor had no clue that he was under such scrutiny. This was something that Holmes had perfected, successfully hiding any attempts he made at observation even from criminals themselves.

His thorough yet discreet body scan method was the ultimate weapon, giving him enough clues and information to draw inferences from and make sturdy conclusions about a person's character, behavior, and tendencies.

Executing a Quick Scan

The purpose of the body scan method is to collect as much information about a person as possible *without* giving yourself away. The last thing you would want is for someone to detect that you're trying to scrutinize them, which would likely urge them to become guarded.

That said, it's vital that you execute the strategy in a tactful, strategic, and efficient way in order to get the most information without tipping the person off. In this light, it's appropriate that you understand the importance of using a system or pattern when executing a scan.

The Holistic View

The body scan starts off with a holistic view. During this step, you take in generalized factors of features that the person might manifest. This includes psychomotor activity, clothing, grooming, posture, movement, and verbal clues. There's a lot that you can decipher based on this information alone.

Psychomotor activity refers to what many of us might call *mannerisms*. A twitch of the eye, a need to twiddle the thumbs, nail biting, and tugging at the earlobes are all classic examples of psychomotor activity. So, why is it important to make a note of them?

As the name suggests, psychomotor activity is movement that might seem superficial at a glance, but is actually rooted in some psychological distress or disturbance. For instance, you might not find the need to bite your nails when you're watching TV, but when you've been called into your boss' office, then it might be a completely different story.

Often, these 'mannerisms' shed light on a person's current emotional state. Those that are closer to distress - like sadness, nervousness, fear, and anxiety - will all manifest some sort of psychomotor activity that the person might not be readily aware of.

Clothing can be trickier to assess because of the way that it might change depending on the situation. On top of that, we all have our own fashion and style preferences, so clothing choices tend to differ widely from person to person.

When scanning clothing, take into consideration the quality of the pieces (are they expensive, branded items?), the wear (do they seem like they're worn often?), style (is it revealing, conservative, traditional, outlandish?), and the cohesiveness of the outfit (do the items match?).

You can tell a lot about a person based on how well they're dressed. People who place particular emphasis on their image will likely throw everything else out the window to guarantee a polished appearance. Others who have limited time or resources might skimp out on clothing and settle for simply looking decent.

Posture has a lot to do with confidence, and is often the first thing people notice when seeing a new individual. A slouched, posture with arms pulled towards the sides or the center of the body showcases a shy, reserved, timid personality. These people might not be too comfortable being in social situations, and may feel guarded when meeting new people.

On the other hand, people who walk and stand with a straight back, who draw the hands away from the midline to assume a more open aura are considered more confident, not afraid to let other people in to see who they are.

Movements are also somehow connected to confidence, but they might also relate to how interested a person is in a specific topic. For instance, someone who particularly enjoys talking about world history might use exaggerated hand movements to bring a point across. Someone who might not be too interested in history might slump back in their chair and just let you do the talking.

A person who moves more readily and naturally is often seen to be more confident in themselves. Someone who chooses to assume a more stagnant countenance might be subconsciously trying to guard themselves to prevent other people from being able to penetrate through their personality.

Verbal clues exist not only in the content of what a person says, but in its delivery. A shaky voice amid nervous laughs and flustered speech could signal nervousness or surprise. Slow, deliberate talking littered with 'uhm' and 'uhh' could be indicative of an in-depth thought process happening behind the scenes.

Stammering is another verbal clue that you might want to consider. Some people, when fabricating a lie, might stammer between words out of nervousness. Fast talking could indicate a need for control and dominance as an individual attempts to get all their points across without giving any other person the opportunity to interject.

Face and Eyes

The face and eyes can give away a lot about a person. Many of the parts of our faces are designed to show emotions, which is why it's important to make sure you're paying attention to the right features when you're meeting someone and trying to decode them.

The **brows** are a great place to start, since these are often the most expressive parts of the face.

298

Furrowed or a raised brow betrays internal thoughts of confusion, uncertainty, or skepticism. Gently raised brows with wide eyes can signal concern or mild surprise. Wide eyes and fully raised eyebrows can be indicative of shock.

Eyes that choose to look away even when being talked to might be guarded, nervous, or contemplative. In some cases, eyes that choose to disengage might also be keeping a secret, trying to prevent you from peering into their truth.

Side glancing can be a tricky thing to decode. In some cases, it might be as simple as recall since the eyes tend to 'search' the mind for information to be retrieved. In some cases, however, side glancing can be a sign of denial or disagreement, especially if the person doesn't seem to be pleased with what you're saying.

Arms and Hands

The arms and hands are another important aspect to make a note of. Hand movements will give you a clearer perspective of confidence and level of interest. But it's equally important to notice unintentional hand movements.

Mannerisms often manifest with the hands, and these little jitters are indicative of nervousness or other slight disturbances and distress. When people feel strong emotions but attempt to hide them, it's possible that they might manifest in the form of mannerisms, since the body needs an outlet to be able to relieve the overpowering feelings.

It's also worth noticing *where* the hands travel. For instance, a person who feels the need to keep stretching out kinks on a shirt might be particular about details, someone who keeps scratching or fiddling with their neck might be trying to soothe a wound. Some experts say that a person who keeps having to fix his or her hair during a conversation might be displaying romantic interest.

Legs and Feet

Finally, the legs and feet are the last important aspect of the body to make note of. The large muscles in these parts are often used to manifest excessive psychological distress that might be particularly pronounced. Significant nervousness often presents itself as a shaking leg.

The way the legs and feet are positioned also give away some information about a person's disposition. Feet that are spread slightly apart creates an open impression, which means that an individual is prepared and willing to take on conversation.

It's often normal for the feet to move and sway gently during a conversation, especially if you're seated. But take note of sudden changes in movement as they could indicate a point of interest during your conversation. For instance, a foot that suddenly points downwards as you shift topics might indicate excitement or disdain. You can confirm this by assessing how the person approaches the conversation after the switch.

Maintaining Discretion

The last thing you'd want would be to give yourself away during a body scan. Once the other person picks up on what you're trying to do, they may be prompted to act differently, covering up their true emotions and behaviors to make it hard for you to get a look inside. Remember, people have a tendency to put on masks, and if they feel that their true self is being compromised, they can alter their mask to conceal what's real.

That said, your top priority should be to maintain the secrecy of your method to prevent your target from altering their behavior to throw you off. You can do this by following these steps:

Glide, Don't Fixate

It's easy to see when someone is *fixed* on a certain aspect of your being - whether it's your face, your clothes, your body, or anything else. So as a general rule, you should want to glide with your eyes instead of keeping them fixated on a specific feature.

If you notice something and want to inspect it more accurately, avoid looking at it for a prolonged period of time. Instead, glide your eyes away from your object of interest and return looking at it after a few moments have passed.

Leverage Body Movements

Your own movements can be used as a tool to help you inspect certain aspects of a person's being. Scratching your nose by tipping your head down gives you a moment of opportunity with your eyes away from your target's view. This can provide you the chance to look at other aspects of the person's being, from their legs to their feet.

Another technique that some people use is side glancing. Using your eyes to look away momentarily while you try to 'rack' through your brain for something to say - even if you know precisely what you want to express - can look exceptionally authentic especially if you know how to play your cards right.

Ask Directly

This tactic can be tricky to execute especially because it might tip your target off since it gives away what you're hoping to learn more about. But asking a direct question about something they *obviously* want to be noticed for brings an opportunity for you to inspect something else entirely.

A large piece of jewellery, a loudly printed shirt, newly colored hair, or a fresh pair of duds are all points of interest that can be brought up in conversation. As you ask about them, you might find your target fixated on the item of your inquiry, giving you a few moments to inspect other aspects.

Keep in mind that while it can be effective, asking too many questions about too many different points of interest can be considered odd, and may make your target feel guarded nonetheless. Asking one or two questions at most should give you the right opportunity without blowing your cover.

Chapter 7:

Your Survival Checklist - The Body Scan Method Condensed

"How long is this to last?" asked the inspector finally. "And what is it we are watching for?"

"I have no more notion than you how long it is to last," Holmes answered with some asperity. "If criminals would always schedule their movements like railway trains, it would certainly be more convenient for all of us."

- Sherlock Holmes, The Complete Sherlock Holmes

There is *a lot* to understand about the body scan method, and the meanings of these movements, mannerisms, behaviors, and qualities can change depending on the context they're presented in. On top of that, their interpretation can also change depending on the combinations of different factors that the person manifests.

What makes the body scan method hard to master is the fact that there can be a lot to pay attention to. For someone who isn't quite as experienced with the tactic, it can be a challenge to get everything down in one go, often leading to an unsystematic method that takes up too much time or even tips off the target.

To help you polish your body scan method, try to memorize this checklist to and store it away in your mind palace. The more you use this list, the easier it becomes to recall each item later on, making your body scan much faster and more efficient.

The Body Scan Checklist

General Body Behavior and Appearance

☐ Clothing

- ☐ Grooming

- ☐ Scent/odor

- ☐ Psychomotor activity

- ☐ Verbal clues

- ☐ Breathing patterns

- ☐ Demeanor

- ☐ Posture

- ☐ Movement

Face and Eyes

- ☐ Brow positioning

- ☐ Eye widening/squinting

- ☐ Eye movements

- ☐ Lip movements

- ☐ Lip biting

- ☐ Twitching

- ☐ Unnatural blinking

- ☐ Asymmetry

- ☐ Grinding of the teeth

Arms and Hands

- ☐ Openness (at the sides, crossed over the chest, toward the midline?)

- ☐ Movements (restricted, free, exaggerated?)

- ☐ Mannerisms

- ☐ Fixation (wounds, scars, rashes, clothing?)

- ☐ Grooming (nails)

- ☐ Shoulder height (relaxed, tense?)

- ☐ Skin (scratches, wounds, bruises, other marks?)

Legs and Feet

☐ Openness (facing forwards, slightly apart, facing sideward, kept together?)

☐ Movements (gentle swaying, rigid, sudden change in position?)

☐ Mannerisms (leg shaking, foot tapping?)

☐ Grooming

☐ Skin (scratches, wounds, bruises, other marks?)

Using and Building Your Checklist

Remember that the items on this list are intended to help you recall the parts of the body that you should pay attention to. These items aren't designed to help you *interpret* what to see, but instead serve as a guide so that you know where to look and in what order.

310

As you continue to use your checklist, you will start to notice other facets of a person's being that might be worth taking note of. Adding these items to your list as you go along will help you establish a more personalized checklist.

Once you establish a strong sense of your list, you can then start storing it away in your mental palace. Designating a special room for this entire list can make it easier to retrieve from memory. You might try using a model of yourself in your mind palace with labels on each part of the body that you might want to inspect.

Understanding What You See

What's the point of picking up on all these subtle mannerisms, movements, and behaviors if you can't possibly understand what they mean? Familiarizing yourself with the manifestations of internal feelings and thoughts can make it easier to understand what they mean when presented in a certain way.

Here are some emotions that you might encounter, and how they look when spoken through body language.

Anger

Anger is a strong emotion which is what makes it easier to detect than others. People who feel anger will manifest either direct eye contact without breaking it, or will completely avoid looking you in the eyes. If the latter is true, they might also roll their eyes and raise a brow.

Someone who feels anger might also bite hard, making the jawlines more prominent. The face will assume a neutral, somewhat bored expression if the individual is attempting to suppress the emotion. In cases when anger might be overwhelming, the eyes are likely to widen and the nostrils may flare. When speaking, an angry person's voice might shake and become louder. The body may tense up and square off to face you completely. Psychomotor activity such as shaking the leg, or fidgeting with the hands may be present.

Disgust

A person who feels disgusted by something might wrinkle the nose and squint the eyes. In cases when they might want to suppress the expression, the eyes might widen slightly and the lips might twitch at one corner. The body - or a part of it - might tense temporarily. The fingers might stretch out as if in an attempt to avoid *touching* the idea of what is deemed disgusting.

Surprise

A sudden lock of the shoulders can signify significant surprise. Eyes may widen and the eyebrows are likely to fully raise. In some cases, the lips may part or may fully open. Some people also tend to use one hand to cover the mouth. Any psychomotor activity or mannerisms may cease temporarily as the person tries to process the unexpected information.

Fear

Fear comes in many forms, and the expression of this emotion can change depending on what causes it. In cases when a person might be trying to conceal the emotion, the lips may stretch horizontally and breathing may become rapid. Psychomotor activity may increase as anxiety starts to take over the system. You may also notice that the person will start to sweat, and they may start stuttering.

Happiness

As one of the most common emotions, it's easy for us to pick up on signs of happiness in a person's demeanor. Increased frequency of hand movements and gestures, widened eyes, smiling lips, and increased verbalization are all common signs of happiness. More subtle ways that happiness might show include slightly wider eyes, slightly raised brows, and increased psychomotor activity especially involving the legs.

Sadness

There's some stigma against sadness, and people are often convinced that it's something they should strive to hide. So sadness is typically suppressed, making it harder to decode compared to many other emotions.

Sadness has a tendency to cause an increased breathing rate, so people will try to normalize that by breathing deeper. This makes for a pronounced rising and falling of the chest as they put effort into trying to control the emotion. Sadness can also cause the corners of the lips to point slightly downwards.

A person might also choose to speak less as they try to regulate the feeling, so verbalizations might be reduced to single-word statements. Psychomotor activity may be completely absent or may be reduced to a gentle, rhythmic motion.

The spectrum of human emotion is definitely extensive, so there are far more to decode than just those enumerated in this list. That said, it's important that you continue to hone your skills and practice your technique in order to become more efficient at identifying the different emotions in the spectrum.

Similarly, you also need to be aware that feelings tend to overlap. Often, these emotions won't exist exclusively, so you need to figure out how they might manifest together.

The Purpose of Knowing

What's the importance of knowing how someone feels internally? Why do you need to pick up on emotions when trying to decode someone? The purpose of knowing is closely linked to the role that emotions play when it comes to behavior.

Revisiting the scenario of the angry boss, you'll notice that the way he felt played a pivotal role in his reaction to your report. Had he been less angry, then he might not have exploded the way that he did.

Knowing how a person *feels* will give you a better idea as to how they might behave in the present situation. This can help you tailor your approach so as to generate the most ideal interaction outcomes.

Conclusion

"A strange enigma is man."

- Sherlock Holmes, The Sign of Four

In our modern day and age, it can be exceptionally difficult to adapt Holmesian techniques because of the many different distractions and excesses that our culture teaches us to cling to. These factors have made it a challenge to decode people because of the mental clutter they create, making room for arguments, misunderstandings, and miscommunication.

While it's not a farfetched idea to think that perhaps Sherlock himself would have trouble understanding people in modern times, many of his skills are still relevant and effective tools to help reduce inefficient social interaction.

Whether it's for romance, for work, for family, or for friendships, there is a great benefit to knowing *how to read people*. This indispensable skill opens the doors to seamless communication and interaction, letting you get the best out of each encounter and mitigate possible disagreements.

We all want to live lives that have as little stress as possible, and learning how to decode the people around you can clear your social life of unwanted distress and difficulty.

So while you might not be able to use these skills exactly the same way Holmes did in his many exploits, they can still prove to be worthy additions to your mental toolbox to give you an edge and improve the way you go through everyday life.

How To Analyze People 4

Inside The Mind Of A Master Detective

Secret Insights About His Mindset And
How He Thinks

-

Including DIY-Exercises

By Patrick Lightman

Introduction

"If we could fly out of that window hand-in-hand, hover over this great city, gently remove the roofs, and peep in at the queer things which are going on, the strange coincidences, the plannings, the cross-purposes, the wonderful chains of events, working through generations, and leading to the most outre results, it would make all fiction with its conventionalities and foreseen conclusions most stale and unprofitable."

\- Sherlock Holmes, The Complete Adventures of Sherlock Holmes

When it comes to exercising the full analytical, deductive, and logical capabilities of the mind, there is no-one quite as iconic as Sherlock Holmes. Despite being a fictional character born of the creativity and fantasy of Arthur Conan Doyle, Holmes has become a household name and a synonym for 'super sleuth'.

Through his adventures, Sherlock was able to wow and impress readers and viewers all over the globe with his impeccable and often seemingly otherworldly capacity to decipher even the most cryptic of clues. In many cases, he found evidence and answers where many others saw nothing.

If you've ever seen a Sherlock Holmes movie or TV show, or if you've ever had your nose stuck in his books, then you might have found yourself wondering - *how does he do it?* Needless to say, Sherlock's astounding detective and investigative capabilities seem alien, yet admirable, making many of us want to achieve the same capacity for thinking - if not for catching crooks, then for getting ahead in everyday life.

Fortunately, the science of Holmes' mind doesn't have to stay a mystery, and the keys to his cognitive skills are in this very guide.

These days, an average everyday person might not

be able to use Sherlock logic for the same, exciting reasons that Holmes did, but, unlocking those skills can help with a variety of daily challenges from work, to school, relationships, finances, and everything in between.

The ability to decipher people and situations, regardless of whether or not they are familiar to you, can help you make the right choices at the right time, as well as avoid and mitigate risks. Thinking like a super sleuth can also make you a much more efficient worker - seeing outcomes before they happen and making the best decisions to reach optimal results without wasting too much time.

Sherlock Holmes once said, *"To a great mind, nothing is little."* So, if you're ready to see the bigger picture in the everyday instances you experience, if you're hoping to get the most out of each opportunity, if you want to protect yourself from potentially harmful people and situations, then your answer is here.

Learn how to mold your mentality to be as great as

Holmes and become the master of your mind by diving into this comprehensive guide.

Chapter 1:

A Powerful Mind Is A Quiet Mind

"My name is Sherlock Holmes. It is my business to know what other people do not know."

- Sherlock Holmes, Adventure of Blue Carbuncle

The year is 1881. Sherlock Holmes and his faithful assistant John H. Watson find themselves in an abandoned home off of Brixton Road. Inside is a bloody crime scene and the body of one Enoch Drebber - lifeless and sprawled across the floor. The investigator discovers upon inspection, however, that there are no wounds on the body.

There were no other clues at the scene of the crime aside from a few documents indicating that Drebber was in London with his secretary, Joseph Srangerson. Upon moving the body, Holmes discovered a single gold wedding band resting underneath. Above the body, written in blood, is the word "RACHE".

With such scant evidence, police at the scene couldn't quite understand where to begin, but Sherlock was already miles ahead. The master investigator gave out a list of characteristics, profiling the assailant and giving police their first lead. Holmes described a man of about 6 feet tall, having disproportionately small feet, and a flushed complexion. He also claimed that the man arrived in a cab with a horse having 3 old shoes and 1 new one.

While the police were busy with their own suspect who was currently apprehended and taken into custody on circumstantial evidence, Holmes and Watson were busy with their own investigation. They were able to cuff and apprehend one Jefferson Hope - a man the police would have never suspected. Fortunately for Sherlock, the man willingly confessed, putting the entire case to rest.

The ring was his sweetheart's and his motive was

passion. Drebber had forced Hope's lady into marriage, and the woman died soon after. Hope felt it was his responsibility to avenge the wife he never had, so he stalked into Drebber's home, stole the ring, and followed the man on his trip to London. There, he intoxicated Drebber, brought him to the abandoned home, and poisoned him.

After he had done the deed, he wrote the word 'RACHE', the German word for revenge, over the body. The blood at the crime scene was his own, brought about by a nosebleed he experienced during the murder - a result of an aneurysm he had suffered as a result of the death of his lady love.

Needless to say, it was thanks to Sherlock's distinct thought process that led to the apprehension of the real murderer, and that iconic story was the beginning of what would be one of the most prominent characters in investigative fiction.

Who Was Sherlock Holmes?

Anyone who enjoys their fair share of investigative fiction should be particularly familiar with Sherlock Holmes. First published in 1886, the stories of Holmes were the brainchild of Arthur Conan Doyle - a physician turned fiction novel writer.

During his time studying at Edinburgh University, Conan Doyle met Dr. Joseph Bell who would become his professor and mentor in forensic medicine. Bell was a renowned forensic scientist, and he inspired Conan Doyle with his sharp wit and unconventional reasoning which led to his prominence in his field.

Deeply impressed by his professor, Conan Doyle decided to work alongside Dr. Bell at the Edinburgh Royal Infirmary after completing his education towards becoming a physician. Here, he would learn more about Bell's thought process - most notable of which was his capability to draw large sweeping conclusions, given even the smallest evidence or information.

The way that Dr. Bell was able to come up with accurate deductions from information that seemed irrelevant or unimportant to most others astounded Conan Doyle, and pushed him to create his own fiction series based on his mentor.

Sherlock Holmes was largely inspired by the totality of Dr. Bell's personality and professional skill. The man would often disregard social mores, was typically uninterested in everyday mundanities, and relied mainly on psychology to solve his cases. In fact, Doyle was so astounded that these were all characteristics used to create Holmes' iconic personality.

While Conan Doyle didn't focus too much on writing Sherlock's history, it is known that the character was born sometime in 1854. Details of his parents were scarce, but the character has been noted to mention that his ancestors were squires in the country. Throughout the series, he mentioned one sibling - a brother in a government position.

Sherlock Holmes has always preferred isolation;

however, due to financial troubles, he was forced to accept John H. Watson as a co-tenant in a shared lodging on 221B Baker Street. Watson would become an indispensable character in the Sherlock Holmes stories, offering insight and practical advice from a conventional thought process that most people have. He was often the voice of reason, tempering Sherlock's outlandish ideas with his empirical points of view.

Watson was often used as a literary device, designated the role of narrator throughout the books. Conan Doyle used his persona to provide readers with insight and an understanding regarding Sherlock's deeper nature, making it easier to decipher how he operated compared to someone more traditional and typical in thinking and reason.

Sherlock would often introduce himself as a 'consulting detective.' He would work hand-in-hand with authorities to apprehend and convict criminals involved in some of the most flustering cases in London. He was also known to work directly with clients who felt he was more skilled and capable to handle their cases than the local police. More often, however, Holmes would try to avoid publicity and was typically happy to have the authorities take full credit for the work he completed.

Sherlock Holmes had a variety of skills in his arsenal, stemming from a deep understanding on numerous topics - both academic and trivial. This exceeding intelligence that's considered far greater than what most people possess is what gave him an edge over most detectives, allowing him to decipher and decode clues and messages, even those inspired by foreign sources - like the RACHE inscription in the story 'A Study in Scarlet'.

In this first novel, Watson observed Holmes and made a list of the topics that the master detective seemed well-versed in. He concluded that geology, chemistry, anatomy, sensationalism, and practical botany were some of his strongest suits. Literature, politics, and astronomy, however, were not.

However, in typical Sherlock fashion, the super sleuth was already two steps ahead of Watson, knowing that the doctor was profiling him, so he pretended not to know anything on certain topics, misleading Dr. Watson and later disproving him in subsequent books in the series. This was all part of Sherlock's preference to remain a mystery to the people around him, making it difficult for anyone to truly understand the extent of his knowledge and logic.

The Super Sleuth's Silent Mind

Aside from his potent repertoire in science, maths, literature, and pop culture, Sherlock Holmes had another efficient tool that became particularly helpful in his crime-solving career - his silent, diligent, and meticulous mind. Consider this quote from one of the most popular Sherlock Holmes novels, 'A Study in Scarlet':

"A fool takes in all the lumber of every sort that he comes across, so that the knowledge which might be useful to him gets crowded out... so that he has difficulty in laying his hands on it. Now the skillful workman is very careful indeed as to what he takes into his brain attic."

What made Sherlock exceptionally skilled at picking out small details and drawing large conclusions was his silent and uncrowded mind. Most of us who use conventional methods of deduction and reason would take every bit of information we could, thinking that a vast collection of data would be more helpful than just having a few pieces of information.

However, Sherlock *knew* where to look, allowing him to discard data that would become nothing more than mental clutter. With this clarity of mind, he was able to see the bigger picture and assess finer details that many others would overlook.

This process of thinking wasn't any different from the thought process of Dr. Bell. The forensic doctor was noted saying that his successful diagnoses were mostly the result of a principle that he applied to his logical process: "Observe carefully, deduce shrewdly, and confirm with evidence."

A calm, collected, and clear mental state helps to relieve the mind of unnecessary information that would steal our attention and draw us away from details that truly matter. Understanding how to leverage a silent mind will highlight information that would seem otherwise unimportant.

Aside from that, Sherlock Holmes also had a knack for doing away with subconscious bias. Most people are impressionable, unconsciously following paths based on information that they've been exposed to in the past. For instance, one investigator who handled a previous murder case might unknowingly handle his next case using the principles he applied in the former.

Unfortunately, this type of bias can be misleading because no two circumstances are ever completely the same. By adapting Holmes' capability to treat each case uniquely and without the use of patterned behavior and decision-making, then details and important pieces of information become far more prominent because you're not forced to *look* where bias tells you to.

In essence, training yourself to think like Holmes means training your mind to adapt a relative clarity when dealing with tricky situations. Avoiding overloading yourself with information that might not matter, focusing on the minute details that are important to the situation, and clearing your thoughts of any possible bias can help turn your traditional thought process into a class A super sleuth skill.

Chapter 2:

Where To Go From There - Sherlock's Mental Toolbox

"I am a brain, Watson. The rest of me is a mere appendix."

- Sherlock Holmes, The Adventure of Mazarin Stone

Sherlock's astounding investigative skills are a manifestation of the tools inside his mental toolbox. These devices are taken and used in combination with one another, sharpening his mind and allowing him to achieve reason and logic far superior to anyone in his day and age - perhaps even anyone in the present.

While his knowledge and his clarity are the cornerstones of his skill, his mental toolbox contains the keys he uses on locked doors and questions that no-one else can answer.

So, what exactly can you find inside Sherlock Holmes' impressive cognitive arsenal? Let's take a peek.

Critical Thinking

While there are a number of different definitions for 'critical thinking', its meaning in the context of Holmes' skills is quite clear. It's the ability to take objective information from a variety of sources to link them together and come to a conclusion. In many ways, critical thinking can be thought of as the opposite of deductive reasoning (which we will discuss more later on).

For Holmes, critical thinking came in handy when piecing together the picture of a crime scene. In the book *The Adventures of Sherlock Holmes* - a compilation of twelve short stories - Sherlock proudly displays his impeccable critical thinking skills in the story *The Boscombe Valley Mystery*.

The narrative discusses the murder of one Charles McCarthy for which his son James was wrongfully convicted. Holmes works to piece together the clues of the crime, starting first by inspecting the boots of both the father and his son - a move that seemed unconventional and irrational to Lestrade, the police officer working on the same case.

Upon inspecting both boots in detail, Sherlock visits the forest where Charles was killed, and immediately concludes that there was a third person at the scene of the crime because there were 3 sets of boot prints on the ground.

Holmes was also able to claim that the assailant was left-handed because of the way that Charles' head had been struck. Given the inconsistency of the footprints on the ground, Holmes was able to conclude that the man responsible for the murder walked with a limp.

Lastly, James claimed that as his father died in his arms, his last words seemed to be a reference to a rat. Sherlock found this interesting, since Charles

338

was heard shouting "cooee" prior to his death, seemingly trying to call out to someone he was intended to meet by the pool. Sherlock surmised that perhaps his last word 'rat' wasn't a word at all, but was instead the last syllable of the word 'Ballarat', the name of a place and a prominent gang from Australia.

Piecing together this information, the detective duo were able to pin down John Turner - a major landowner in Boscombe Valley. He had been part of an Australian gang which hijacked a gold convoy on which Charles was the wagon driver. He spared Charles' life despite knowing that he could later tell the police of Turner's involvement in the heist.

Turner soon left the gang and started a new life. When he came across Charles by chance in Boscombe Valley, Charles threatened him with blackmail, demanding land and riches in exchange for his silence. Soon, Charles also made demands to marry his son James to John Turner's daughter, Alice.

Unfortunately, this was the last straw for John, not wanting his family to be tainted by Charles, so he decided to meet the man at the pool, where he waited for James to leave; after which, he killed Charles with a single strike to the left temple.

While many of us wouldn't know where to begin in this particular case, Sherlock Holmes was able to choose the appropriate entry point to properly dissect the information he was initially given. Knowing that the crime was committed on soil, he knew that there would be prints left behind, and proving that there was more than one person at the scene would exonerate James.

Details such as the location of the wound on the victim's body, the pressure of the footsteps on the soil, and the victim's last words, all seemed like disconnected bits of information; However, to a super sleuth like Holmes, they were all indicative of a single assailant, providing the detective with an excess of information that he could use to provide authorities with a clear profile of the real murderer.

Holmes' Mind Palace

The method of loci is an old memorization tool that was first used in ancient Roman and Greek rhetorical treatises. The method was widely used prior to the popularization of print, since it was an effective method for mentally storing information.

The technique works by creating a mental 'palace' - an architectural visualization of a house, a building, a mansion, a street lined with houses, or whatever else you might fancy. More often than not, people choose familiar places for their mental palace, typically utilizing the image of a childhood home since it is easier to remember each room and compartment in a place you've already physically seen.

Once the appearance of the palace has been decided, the individual will then designate a specific idea to each room. For instance, a person who needs to remember to pick up milk at the grocery store might designate a room in the house to the visualization of milk. It's encouraged that representations be outlandish and phantasmagorical to make them easier to remember, so you might use the image of a large dancing carton of milk upon opening that specific door so that the memory sticks.

Of course, Holmes used his mental palace for far more important items than just the things he had to tick off of his grocery list, but the purpose was essentially the same, and that was to improve his memory capacity.

Keeping Only *What's Important*

In *A Study in Scarlet,* Watson was surprised to learn that Holmes wasn't aware that the Earth revolved around the sun, considering the man's intellect, but Holmes was quick to clarify that it wasn't that he didn't know the information, just that he didn't find the purpose to remember it.

"You say we go round the sun. If we went round

the moon, it would not make a pennyworth of difference to me or to my work," Sherlock was famously quoted for.

With that, we can deduce that the master investigator only made room for specific items in his mind palace. Despite knowledge of the Earth's revolution being based on real, scientific evidence, Sherlock had no need for it. This means that he only reserved rooms in his memory bank for concepts that he needed on a daily basis. This runs contrary to the way most of us would use our memory, usually littering the space with sentimental items that serve no practical or future purpose.

The Mental Attic

You might say that the mental attic is another room in the mind palace, and in a lot of ways, the concepts can overlap. In fact, some people have suggested that when Holmes refers to his mental attic, he's actually pertaining to his mind palace, but there are distinctions between the two spaces.

While the palace serves the purpose of a memory bank, the mental attic is where you take specific pieces of information to be broken down, dissected, inspected, and studied in detail. This is where you might bring other tools to help bring answers to light, or to make better sense of a specific topic or problem.

Unlike the rest of your mind palace which might have to be decorated and detailed, the mental attic should be clear, clutter-free, and clean. In many ways, the mental attic might be the representation of your cognitive clarity - one of the cornerstones of Holmes' unique skills.

Having a clear mental attic can provide you with the ideal cognitive space to inspect specific details and information more closely without any other ideas or concepts getting in the way. Sherlock was often noted talking about his mental attic - a clutter-free space where he would bring lumber to craft. The clearer the attic, the easier it would be to work on new ideas, concepts, and decisions.

Deductive Reasoning

Deductive reasoning is a concept used to arrive at a valid, verifiable reality. It happens when an individual uses the 'top-down' approach to arrive at a conclusion based on available information and evidence.

For instance, Sherlock visits a crime scene having been briefed by police on what happened at the location. The master investigator knows that they're dealing with a murder case, but they need to know specifics - how and why it was done, as well as who did it.

Visiting the location to find clues, Sherlock would use deductive reasoning to figure out how the different pieces of the crime scene fit the premise of murder. In essence, **_deductive reasoning describes the process of working with a general idea or hypothesis and then using that to guide the interpretation of smaller observations_**.

Consider this scenario:

Authorities are informed that several women in a low income neighborhood have been harrassed by a midnight bed intruder.

They discover the same finger prints at all crime scenes despite the victims not being acquianted with one another.

The authorities run the prints through the sex offender database and find a match

The man is identified, and he is subsequently apprehended and charged with sexual harrassment and burglary.

In this example, the authorities are operating on a proven piece of knowledge - that an individual had been entering houses in the small hours of the morning, and sexually harassing women as they slept. This has been verified because of the numerous accounts of women with similar stories in the same area.

Given this information, authorities brushed through the homes of the victims to search for possible clues. They found the same set of fingerprints inside every home, despite none of the victims not knowing each other, thus making it impossible for them to leave their prints in each other' s homes.

The premise was that the same individual was responsible for all of the cases, so authorities deduced that the fingerprints left behind all belonged to the same person. Given the nature of his crime, it was fitting to search for him through the sex offender database, where the authorities were able to find a match.

Deductive reasoning allowed authorities to find clues that matched the original premise, drawing smaller conclusions from one general idea.

Inductive Reasoning

Despite being particularly gifted when it came to deductive reasoning, the logical thought pattern that made Sherlock Holmes particularly popular was his capacity for inductive reasoning. Considered the complete opposite of deductive reasoning, induction is the process of taking smaller pieces of information and then drawing one generalized conclusion by connecting the dots.

Inductive reasoning can be far more challenging because there could be a number of possibilities at the end of a trail. What's more, some cases might not make sense unless you have all of the smaller details, much like a puzzle that won't create a full image if you lose some of the pieces.

Holmes constantly wowed his Watson, the authorities, and the general public with his superb inductive logic. For instance, in the iconic first novel *A Study in Scarlet,* Holmes was able to come up with a profile for Enoch Drebber's assailant based on nothing more than the scant evidence at the scene.

Sherlock claimed that the murderer was a tall man, 6 feet in height, that he had long nails on his right hand, a flushed complexion, impeccably small feet for his size, and that he arrived in a cab with a horse that had 3 new shoes and 1 old one. How exactly did Holmes come to conclude all of these characteristics?

While it's unclear and definitely baffling to think of how Sherlock might have determined the suspect's profile, we can infer that he merely used bits and pieces of information at the scene to develop an image of the assailant. At the end of the story, when the man responsible was apprehended, it was discovered that he looked *exactly* as Holmes had described him and that he did in fact, have a horse with 3 old shoes.

To further clarify the process of inductive reasoning, consider this chain of events.

Police are informed of a man found dead in his apartment. The body had decomposed, causing a stench to flow through the neighboring units, which is ultimately what made other tenants find the source.

The cause of the man's death is unclear and evidence at the scene is limited. Upon checking all doors and entry points, it's assumed that there was no foul play.

The body is brought to the lab for inspection. Several needle wounds are found over the forearm, and there are traces of narcotics in the body's system.

The death is ruled as an overdose.

Upon arriving at the scene, police are given no

information other than the fact that there is a dead body in the unit. Using the evidence found in the apartment, police officers *rule out* possible reasons such as murder or burglary. This narrows down the probable causes for the man's death, until they're able to piece evidence together to conclude overdose.

Essentially, the main difference between deductive and inductive reasoning is that, when using the former, individuals work to find pieces that fit a proven outcome. "This man was murdered, how was it done and who did it?" The objective is to find the clues that further justify the conclusion.

With inductive reasoning, the process starts with the pieces of the puzzle which are then formed together to come up with the result. "We found these clues at the scene of the crime. What do they mean, and how do they explain what happened to this victim?" The objective is to put together evidence in order to draw a conclusion.

Meditation

Having been around for centuries, meditation is a practice that's common to most eastern religions. This process of calming the mind and thinking on a deeper level about certain concepts and events is known to provide people with a complete perspective. This helps individuals make far more intuitive decisions by inspecting all the angles of a situation.

Often, when we hear the word 'meditation', we tend to think about people sitting on a yoga mat with their legs crossed, holding their hands in an 'Om' position. While Sherlock did meditate, Conan Doyle didn't describe him adapting to this particular practice. In fact, the author never truly made mention of the word 'meditation' throughout his series of books.

Despite this, we can deduce that he did in fact meditate, although not following the traditional methods that we know. In many cases, Watson would talk about finding Sherlock frozen, dazed, and zoned out, in the same position he had been in hours before when Watson left their lodgings.

During these moments, Holmes would be deep in thought, thinking of the many different possibilities and answers to the mystery he was currently working on. In essence, he was *meditating* or ruminating deeply to uncover facts and clues that he might have overlooked during the investigation.

Metathinking

You'd think that 'thinking about thinking' would cause nothing but a headache, but the process can actually help sharpen the mind. Taking the time to process the way your own cognition works can shed light on ineffective thinking processes that can be improved to become more efficient.

While there aren't any direct references to metacognition in the Sherlock Holmes series, the super sleuth does talk about his own mental process which leads readers to understand that Holmes is constantly trying to improve his thinking in order to become more efficient at his trade.

Metathinking takes a lot more than what many of us might assume. Developing a higher level of cognitive capabilities by thinking about your own process is prone to a lot of bias, since many of us may find it difficult to perceive errors or inefficiencies in our own thought process.

In many ways, it's comparable to looking at yourself in a mirror face-to-face, with nothing more than an inch separating your skin from the reflective surface. It becomes hard to see the whole picture, and almost impossible to understand whether there are any problems with the way you're dressed.

Despite the challenge, incorporating metathinking into your arsenal can help significantly improve the way you surpass daily challenges. It can be particularly helpful when you reach a dead end, allowing you to restructure the way you approach a situation so you can find a solution that might not have been as apparent the first time.

Chapter 3:

The Art Of Asking The Right Questions

"Is there any point to which you would wish to draw my attention?'

'To the curious incident of the dog in the night-time.'

'The dog did nothing in the night-time.'

'That was the curious incident,' remarked Sherlock Holmes."

- Sherlock Holmes, Silver Blaze

Sherlock Holmes had a knack for asking long lists of unconventional questions that would usually raise the eyebrows of the officials that worked alongside him. The super sleuth was known to make a habit of asking questions that, at times, seemed unreasonable and unimportant to most because they either seemed like they had obvious answers or that they were irrelevant to the case.

Anyone who knew Sherlock, however, knew that to him, *there was nothing more deceptive than an obvious fact.*

The master detective's critical thinking prowess was of course, worthy of praise and admiration. It was through his incredible capacity to ask the right questions that he was able to solve his cases with utmost precision and speed, compared to many other trained professionals that would work with him.

In daily life, being able to ask the right questions at the right time can mean the difference between success and failure. Whether it's at work, at school, or at home, choosing to dwell on the right train of thought instead of dealing with musings that might not be beneficial or relevant later on, can save time, money, and even mitigate risks.

The Dangers of Disorganized Thinking

The year is 2003. An Airbus A300B4-200F cargo plane operated by DHL had just departed from Baghdad, Iraq on its way to Bahrain. The Airbus was manned by an experienced flight crew of 3, with a total of 17,925 hours of flight experience between them.

Their aircraft was carrying packages handled by the DHL company, and was working on a routine schedule to deliver cargo. The crew executed a rapid climbout since they were operating in dangerous territory. The quick ascent was intended to reduce their exposure to a ground attack.

Unfortunately, at about 8,000 feet, the Airbus was struck by a surface-to-air missile which collided with the left wing. The damage destroyed their primary fuel tank, which ultimately caused the affected wing to catch fire. Needless to say, the aircraft was acting unpredictably, making it increasingly difficult for the men on board to take control.

Within 10 minutes of the strike, the 3 men on board were able to learn how to manage turns, ascents, and most importantly, descents. After executing a tight right turn, they calculated trajectory and decided to land back in the terminal where they took off.

The entire incident was over in 16 minutes, with all 3 men walking away scot-free. They were handed awards for their bravery and quick thinking which managed to help save their cargo, and contributed deeply to our modern understanding of flight safety.

Were these 3 men disorganized thinkers?

Quite the contrary, the crew of the iconic 2003 Baghdad DHL attempted shootdown incident put some awesome critical thinking into action during those moments of distress. Thanks to their presence of mind and quick analysis, they were able to come up with a plan to save their plane and their lives.

In contrast, a disorganized thinker might have abandoned the plane at the moment of the strike. How could this have turned out? Knowing that there were grounded threats that were out to cause harm, it's possible that jumping out of the plane with a conspicuous parachute might attract attention and cause further violence.

On top of that, leaving the burning plane mid-flight meant there would be no way to determine, or control, where it might crash. This could place hundreds (if not thousands) of civilians at risk, as well as compromise the safety and integrity of the cargo on board.

Funny enough, place most people in a hypothetical situation concerning a burning plane, and they'll give you a *disorganized response*. Many would choose to jump out and abandon the aircraft, and some might even say that the first thing they'd do would be to phone a loved one.

Maybe it's because not everyone is trained in handling aircraft emergencies, which is why we typically resort to unsystematic solutions. *Not knowing the right questions to ask given a specific situation can result in dangerous and even life-threatening outcomes.*

The Process of Critical Thinking

Unlike disorganized thought which tends to disregard any patterns, reason, or logic, critical thinking is the process of thinking *with and on purpose.* The cogs in your brain are operated and manipulated following specific, logical, and purposeful trends and patterns to help you arrive at a reasonable, reliable conclusion that can be practically applied with predictable outcomes.

There are different facets to critical thinking, and

these 7 aspects are used in combination to generate the best possible solution for a given problem:

1. **Analysis** - The process of breaking down a concept or topic in order to further understand how it relates to other concepts, how it works, and what it is.

2. **Applying standards** - Using pre-established standards from different bodies of knowledge in order to assess how a specific concept or idea fits or strays from these universally accepted truths.

3. **Discrimination** - Comparing and contrasting two or more concepts or ideas to find out how they differ and how they're similar to one another. This may also involve ranking variables or separating them into organized categories.

4. **Information seeking** - Systematically seeking evidence or information from relevant, reliable sources in order to support

a study or to find possible solutions for a given problem.

5. **Logic** - Drawing conclusions or making inferences based on information that's supported by facts and reliable evidence.

6. **Prediction** - Heavily used by the men in the iconic 2003 DHL flight, prediction is the capacity to think of a plan and envision the possible consequences that might come with it. This may also include weighing the pros and cons associated with different possible plans, and choosing the one with the most limited risks.

7. **Transforming knowledge** - Improving, adapting, or evolving known information to enhance its usefulness in a given situation.

Real-Life Applications of Critical Thinking

Whether it's an annual report for work or a final project for a major subject, there are a variety of applications for critical thinking. This important cognitive tool can improve not only your own personal capabilities towards understanding truths and mysteries around you, but also help you become a more sensible conversationalist.

Some of the questions guided by critical thinking have limitless uses and can be applied even in daily conversation. For anyone trying to sharpen their mind and think more like Sherlock, using these open-ended questions when necessary and possible, can help make for much more meaningful daily encounters.

Sample Questions to Fuel Critical Thinking

WHO	...will benefit from this?
	...might be negatively impacted by this?
	...might be able to provide deeper insight?

	...might prefer a different course of action?
	...do we need in order to execute this plan?
	...can provide unique skills for this?
WHEN	...might this cause harm?
	...would be the best time to execute this plan?
	...can we know that we've been successful?
	...should we execute a contingency plan?
	...can we expect this situation to change?
	...can we start to anticipate the benefits?
WHERE	...would this be most beneficial?
	...is there the greatest need for this plan?
	...can we seek out more information?
	...are the facts of this that could possibly use improvement?
	...else has this been done before?
	...else might this type of problem exist?
WHAT	...could be the best/worst outcome?
	...might be a better alternative?
	...can be changed?

	...might be a possible counter argument for this?
	...can be gained from this?
WHY	...is this challenging?
	...do we need to solve this?
	...should this be addressed in this manner?
	...is this a necessary step?
	...is this a relevant issue?
	...did we arrive at this situation?
HOW	...can we improve this situation?
	...should we approach this problem?
	...will this affect the people involved?
	...will this change the current conditions?
	...does this benefit or harm us?
	...will this turn out?
	...do we know that this is the truth?

Honing Your Inner Holmes - DIY Experiment

Now that you've got a better understanding of how

to use your critical thinking skills, it's time to put them to the test. This short DIY experiment should provide you with the opportunity to exercise your capability to *ask the right questions* so you can arrive at the best possible solution for each situation.

Instructions: You will be presented with a situational problem with multiple choice answers. Choose the option that best suits your course of action based on the issue presented. While there is no right or wrong answer, there are specific choices that may reach more ideal outcomes given the specific problem. The top answers and the explanation for each will be listed at the end of the quiz.

You're working as a retail manager for a bookstore, and a customer walks in to check the items under the history section. After around 15 minutes of going back and forth between the aisles of books, the customer becomes visibly distressed, and you surmise it's because she hasn't found the specific title or topic she's looking for.

You approach her and ask how you can help her, and she says that she's looking for a book by Simon Schama entitled "Citizens: A Chronicle of the French Revolution". To help ease the search, you escort her to your station where you type the title of the book into your inventory database.

Here you find that the book is out of stock. What do you tell your customer?

A. You apologize and tell her that the book is currently unavailable; however, you offer to pre-order the item for her and tell her that you can send her an email once it becomes available.

B. You provide her with the ISBN code for the book and tell her that she can use it to search for the item through the online database that other bookstores have.

C. You tell her that the item might be available in another branch of your bookstore, located around 45 minutes away via car.

1. You're in your final year of college and are tasked to complete one last project for one of your major subjects. The class is divided into groups of 4, and another one of your members is assigned the leader of your group.

It's important that you meet after class hours as a *complete group* to discuss the role that each member will play in your project; however, 2 of your members, as well as the leader, will be partially unavailable for the next 3 weeks since they're both working students.

The first member has Tuesdays and Thursdays off, and the other has Wednesdays and Fridays off. They both work at the local library. On weekends, all members are unavailable due to personal engagements with family.

How can you make sure that everyone will be able to participate in the completion of your project despite the discrepancies in your schedules?

A. Meet at the library after class and ask the members to spare a few minutes between shifts to discuss your project.

B. Ask each member their most convenient and available time, and schedule an online discussion to help improve your project progress.

C. Request that the members all sacrifice at least one weekend so that the group can plan for the project.

2. As you drive through a remote location in the pouring rain, you see a car with blinking hazard lights stopped at the side of the road. A man who appears to have been driving the vehicle is standing beside the car, holding his jacket over his head, and looking in your direction. He waves to signal that he needs assistance.

You recall reading about new reports of people being victimized by a highway robber in this area. The description of the perpetrator, however, doesn't quite fit the appearance of the man you're approaching.

How do you approach this situation?

    A. Don't help. Keep driving and ignore the man.

    B. Stop momentarily beside the man's vehicle and signal him that you're calling for roadside assistance so he can get help, and then drive away.

    C. Stop completely beside the vehicle and slightly crack open your passenger window. Ask him what happened and whether he needs any help.

Answers:

1. The customer in the store is interested in buying a specific title, but is disappointed to find that you currently don't have that title in stock. Here are some critical thinking questions you can ask yourself to arrive at the right solution:

    • What does this customer need? A book.

- Why is she upset?

- What can you do to make sure she gets a copy?

All things considered, the most ideal solution for this specific situation is option **A.** While the other 2 answers might be able to provide her with some assistance, option A gives her a guarantee that she'll definitely have her own copy, albeit not immediately. The other two options will not promise that the customer will be able to purchase the book.

2. The issue in this scenario is the availability of your group members. Because it's imperative that you all meet together to kick off your project plan, you need to make sure that everyone can make time for a group discussion.

- Why can't each member make time after classes?

- What are the alternatives to meeting in person?

- How can you bypass the issue of schedules without disrupting each member's work and school schedule?

In this particular situation, you can choose either option **B or C.** The problem with option A is that it interferes with the 2 members' work schedule, which obviously isn't permissible.

Option B might work given that each member is willing to wake up earlier, to stay up later, in order to be able to execute an online meeting where all the members can participate. Option C might work if members are willing to sacrifice one weekend so that the team can have time to manage the project plan.

3. Your safety is the main concern in this particular situation. The fact that highway robbery has been an issue in this area makes it potentially dangerous to entertain any possible threats to your security. Here are some questions you might want to ask:

- How can I help this person without sacrificing my safety?

- What are the possible ways that I can provide assistance without leaving my vehicle?

- What can I do in case this person does happen to be the perpetrator in the reports?

Given the facts, it's important that you consider your safety and be wary when dealing with the man on the side of the road. The best way to resolve both his situation and keep yourself secure would be to call roadside assistance for him - option **B**.

This way, you've tipped someone of your location in case anything wrong happens, and you've also provided the man with more reliable help given that roadside assistance will arrive with more equipment that might be necessary for the situation.

Chapter 4:

The Mental Attic Concept

"I consider that a man's brain is originally like an empty, little attic, and you have to stock it with furniture as you choose."

- Sherlock Holmes, A Study in Scarlet

The concept of the mental attic is one that Sherlock Holmes regularly references throughout the books. This symbolic space in his mind is where he takes information to dissect, inspect, and analyze in order to come up with his conclusions.

In a lot of ways, the mental attic has been said to work in the same way as the mind palace, however there are minor differences between the 2 spaces. For starters, the mind palace is where memories are stored, while the mental attic is a relatively clear space where information is brought in order to be understood further.

While it might be difficult to fully understand how the concept of the mental attic works, it can be polished and honed in order to give you a more optimal space for interpreting information and data.

The *Qualities* of a Mental Attic

Most people think that the mental attic can be any random 'empty' space they can think of, giving it physical properties and aspects to make it easier to revisit the space at your volition.

Although that is an important aspect of your mental attic space, you need to understand that there's more to developing an attic than simply 'imagining' how it might physically look.

A 'clutter-free' mental space is one that isn't only clear from other ideas and concepts that could interfere with the interpretation of new information, but also free from bias and egocentric tendencies.

What does that mean?

Each one of us has a history, has our own beliefs, our own ideas, and our own values. When trying to dissect information, these concepts can get in the way in the form of a bias, keeping us from truly understanding how a certain event or situation really is.

For instance, imagine you are a religious individual who is assigned to be the head of your congregation. One of your pastors has been accused of infidelity. Because you yourself know that this isn't something you would do given your sturdy moral compass guided by spiritual teachings, you refuse to believe that the pastor in question has committed the allegation.

In this case, your religious obligation on yourself has turned into a bias, making it difficult for you to see that other people, despite their affiliation with the same church, might not have such a strong desire to stick to what you believe is correct.

There are ways that you can improve your own mental attic to make it more conducive for information interpretation. How can that be done? Try out this short experiment:

Honing *Your* Inner Holmes - DIY Experiment

In this exercise, you'll be given a premise, a context, and a problem. Your task is to make sure you're providing the best answers after interpreting all the information in your mental attic. There will be several options for each problem, one of which is a slightly more ideal solution than the other. The objective is to come up with an answer that holds the least bias.

1. You've studied all night for your final exam while your best friend has spent most of his time playing a newly released video game. During the

test, you catch him taking side glances at your paper.

A week later, you receive your test results, and your best friend has scored slightly higher than you. He says thanks for letting him copy off of your answers, although you weren't completely willing to allow him at the time.

What do you do?

A. Tell the professor that your friend cheated off of your answers during the test because it goes against policy.

B. Tell the professor that your friend cheated off of your answers during the test because you feel it is unfair that he got a higher score despite copying off of you.

C. Do nothing. He's your best friend and you don't want to ruin your friendship.

2. You've entered your PIN incorrectly 3 times, and so your account has been temporarily

locked until you can visit your issuing bank branch to have the issue sorted out. Unfortunately, you've only got $40 USD left in your wallet to see you through the next few weeks, since you won't be able to visit your bank until next month given your hectic schedule.

As you walk down the sidewalk, you find a leather coin purse containing over $300 USD in folded bills and coins. You inspect it further and find that there isn't any identification information that you can use to find out who owns the purse.

While you're debating what to do, a homeless person walks up to you and asks if you have anything to spare, even just for a meal. What do you do?

A. Hand the homeless individual a few dollars and keep the rest of the contents of the purse for yourself. This should be enough to help you through the next week until you can visit your specific bank branch.

B. You walk away from the homeless person and keep all the contents of the coin purse to yourself. You need every last dollar for yourself.

C. You decline the homeless person since you don't have any money to give from your own pocket, and visit the nearest police station to surrender the coin purse.

3. You're a kindergarten teacher and it's currently time for your students to have their snacks. As you're helping some of the kids open their lunchboxes, you hear one student cry from the back of the room.

You approach the table and find that her juice had spilled over. She claims that the student next to her was the boy responsible. This student says that he didn't spill the juice on purpose, despite being known to bully other students regularly.

What do you do?

A. Punish the boy and give him a time out. His

reputation makes it more likely that he deliberately spilled the juice.

B. Separate the students and ask each one their account of what happened. Ask other students around their table to find out which story is true.

C. Tell the boy to apologize and be done with it. No use crying over spilled juice.

Answers

1. The best solution for this scenario is option **A.** It's against school policy to cheat regardless of your closeness with the individual who committed the violation. Option B isn't free of bias since you're reporting based on your feelings towards receiving a lower score. Option C is biased since the refusal to report stems from your affiliation with the individual who violated policy.

2. The biases in this situation come in the form

of your need for money and our generalized moral obligation to help the less fortunate. That's why in this case, the correct solution would be option **C**. Despite your situation and the situation of the homeless individual asking for money, it's important that you surrender the coin purse because it belongs to someone else entirely.

3. The reputation of the boy in the situation works as a bias, making it easier for you to assume that the child did it on purpose. That's why option A doesn't make the best solution. In the case of option C, forcing the boy to apologize without truly understanding the role he played in the problem does not benefit all the parties involved because the boy's guilt has not been verified. That's why the best solution would be option **B**.

Chapter 5:

How To Memorize Everything - Holmes' Mind Palace

"It is mistaken to think that that little room has elastic walls and can distend to any extent. Depend upon it there comes a time when for every addition of knowledge, you forget something that you knew before. It is one of the highest importance, therefore, not to have useless facts elbowing out the useful ones."

- Sherlock Holmes, A Study in Scarlet

Different from the mental attic, the mind palace is the storage space for different pertinent concepts and memories that are necessary for future use. Sherlock Holmes was known to keep only the most important information in his mental palace, even going as far as forgetting that the earth revolved around the sun simply because he had no purpose for that information.

These days, people use the concept of the mind palace to help improve their memory. Some professionals have leveraged the strategy in order to memorize speeches, to track company progress, or to help budget finances. Some people use it for everyday tasks like remembering their grocery list. That said, there are infinite applications for the mind palace strategy, making it an indispensable tool for anyone and everyone.

Making Your Own Mind Palace

Remembering specific, important memories or concepts isn't just something for super sleuths; here is how you can build yours:

1. **Engage All Your Senses** - The reason why the mental palace technique works so well is because it engages visual and spatial information that's correlated with specific concepts, but there are ways to help make your palace far more resilient against forgetfulness.

Engaging other senses to create a richer, more unique experience as you mentally walk through your memory bank, allowing a more accurate recall of the concepts you store. For instance, some people like to play specific music or harmonies when trying to construct their mental space. This helps create an atmosphere, making it easier to revisit your structure when you need to pull out a memory.

It's also possible to use different scents to further strengthen the idea of a mental palace. The sense of smell ties closely with memory, which is why you might be reminded of very old places, people, and experiences as far back as your early childhood when you come across a familiar scent.

If you find that you need to visit your palace, simply play the tune or get a whiff of the scent you've chosen to get an accurate recall of the space you've created to store your memories.

2. **Draw the Layout** - If you're structuring your mind palace from scratch, then it might be important that you draw out the layout of the

space. Tracing the different hallways, pathways, stairs, and other features that lead from one room to another, will help guarantee that you don't end up forgetting the specific blueprint of your space.

If you're not keen on drawing, then you may want to consider choosing a palace that resembles a structure that you are already familiar with. Using the layout and aesthetic of your current home, or even your childhood home, should make it easier to remember the different rooms and places inside your memory bank.

3. **Write a Detailed Description of Your Space** - The foundation of an effective mental palace is a structure that you can recall and describe like the back of your hand. If you can't even remember the different rooms in your space, then you might easily forget specific items you place throughout the area.

Aside from drawing a layout of your space, you may also want to consider writing a detailed description of your mind palace. Narratives strengthen our ideas of fiction, making them easier to visualize and remember, so it's important to make sure that you write a description that's particularly in-depth, down to the different colors, textures, and possibly even emotions associated with specific areas in the space.

When writing, try to think of yourself as a novelist describing the setting of a story. Provide as much detail as you can. For instance, you can go as in-depth as talking about chipped paint on a window frame in one of the bedrooms. This helps add character and uniqueness to the space, making it more distinct and easier to recall.

4. **Make as** Many **Unique Associations with Each Room as You Can** - If all of the different rooms down the hallway inside your mind palace feature the same, bland, beige walls and white tiles, then how can you differentiate the first room from the last? Creating distinct aesthetics in each room will help make it easier

to remember which one goes where.

To ease the process of recall, some design the rooms in their mind palace to have different colors and themes. That way, you can more readily remember which rooms come first, and how they are arranged in the space. On top of that, this also makes it easier to remember where you put specific concepts. For example, you might be able to remember a particular memory more readily if you can describe the room where you put it.

5. **Furnish and Design the Space** - Memories and concepts don't need to be stored exclusively in rooms. If that were the case, then you might have *too many rooms in your mind palace* making it hard to remember the blueprint. In the same way, you might also have to keep adding rooms when you find the need to store a new memory.

Instead, you can furnish and decorate the mental representation of your memory, with each piece of furniture or decor corresponding with a specific idea or concept. This way, you can keep your mind palace condensed without having to sacrifice memories and thoughts that might be important to you.

People who have successfully used the mind palace concept also usually recommend that ideas be associated with items in the palace that have similar sounding names. For instance, a student trying to remember all the key people in a history lecture might designate the concept of *George Washington* with a *washing* machine.

When you are using your mind palace, always remember to flow through it as though it were a real place. Some people try to visualize themselves inside a room right away, which can disrupt the memory of the rest of the structure. That said, always enter through the main door, walk through the hallways, and don't skip out any spaces on your way to a specific memory.

If you can, take your time and try to visualize every detail you've written in your description. Visualize paintings you put on the walls, minute details and qualities of the rooms, as well as the different pieces of furniture and decor that you might have used to make your palace more unique.

Honing Your Inner Holmes - DIY Experiment

In this short test, your task is to create a mind palace based on a predetermined grocery list. The layout of the palace, as well as the furnishings, decor and the size are all up to you.

YOUR GROCERY LIST

- Two (2) cartons of milk

- Six (6) single-serve fruit flavored yogurt cups

- Three (3) dozen eggs

- One (1) bottle of shampoo

- Six (6) red apples

- Six (6) green apples

- Two (2) cans of whole peeled tomatoes

- Three (3) cartons of juice (any flavor)

- One (1) 350g bottle of ground coffee

- Two (2) rolls of 3-ply tissue

- Three (3) kilos of ground beef

- Three (3) kilos of beef brisket

Once you're confident that you'd be able to recall each item on the list with minimal effort using your palace, proceed to the following set of questions to test how well you remember the grocery list items.

Questions. Make sure to answer EACH QUESTION before referring back to the original list. Write down your answer to each number. Once you've finished, visit the list and find out how well you were able to remember your list based on your mind palace.

1. How many items are on your list?

2. How many items are non-food items?

3. How many eggs in total are included in your list?

4. How many apples in total are included in your list?

5. TRUE OR FALSE - There are 3 meat products on your list.

6. TRUE OR FALSE - You need 3 rolls of 2-ply tissue.

7. TRUE OR FALSE - Orange juice is included in your list.

8. How many grams of coffee do you need?

1. How many toiletries do you need?

Chapter 6:

The Art Of Deduction - A Step-By-Step Guide

"The man might have died in a fit; but then the jewels are missing," mused the Inspector,

"Ha! I have a theory. These flashes come upon me at times... What do you think of this, Holmes? Sholto was, on his own confession, with his brother last night. The brother died in a fit, on which Sholto walked off the treasure! How's that?"

"On which the dead man very considerately got up and locked the door on the inside," said Holmes."

- Sherlock Holmes, The Sign of Four

Deduction is by far one of Sherlock's most used skills. This process of reasoning entails *taking information* from a previously established fact in order to learn *specific truths*. That is, the process takes **general information** and **turns it into specific information**. That's why it's called *deductive* reasoning, because you deduce details from general fact.

How to Master the Art of Deduction

The skill of deductive reasoning isn't one that's as easily mastered. It takes practice and mindfulness in order to be able to develop this type of logic. Fortunately, we can *deduce* steps to master the art of deduction through Sherlock Holmes' exploits.

1. **Active Listening** - One of the main issues that people have these days is the inability to listen without interfering. In a given situation where you're objective is to find an answer, interjecting with your own opinions can dampen the value of the information

being delivered. This doesn't only apply to verbal interference that you might cause by speaking, but also interference that might occur if you *think* while someone is sharing information.

Despite having a reputation of an eccentric with little regard for social mores, Sherlock Holmes was exceptionally gifted when it came to keen listening. In fact, he was often *too* silent when discussions would occur around him, often with his eyes closed and his fingertips pressed against each other.

The super sleuth had a talent for keeping his mouth and his thoughts quiet when there was new information being delivered to him. This made sure that he would absorb the new details in their entirety without contaminating them with his own thoughts, beliefs, and concepts. It would only be after he received all the pertinent information that he would open his mental toolbox to dissect the details.

2. **Keen Observation** - Sometimes, deducing the details means *looking* for them given the information you already have. Sherlock was often described sitting in his lodgings, staring off into the distance, rethinking information that had already been previously provided.

The process of revisiting information can help bring new details to light, especially if there was some mental clutter preventing a clear view of truth when it was first inspected. Taking all the facets of verified facts into consideration can reveal new information that wasn't there before.

3. **Discuss the Details** - "*Nothing clears up a case so much as stating it to another person.*" John Watson was more than just an assistant to Holmes - he was instrumental in Holmes' detective work. Sherlock would often discuss information with Watson, bouncing his ideas off of the good doctor who was equally intelligent and intuitive.

In cases when some information might not be clear, it could be best to find someone to talk to. This strategy lets you slow down your mental process, puts things into perspective, and might even get you brand new outlooks depending on how someone else sees the situation.

Honing Your Inner Holmes - DIY Experiment

Deductive reasoning can be a powerful tool to learning new truths and coming up with viable solutions to some of the most perplexing situations. Try out this short exercise to find out how sharp your skills are:

For this particular quiz, assume that both statements are *true*. Use them as the premise for your answer. Based on the information they provide, decide which of the following choices could most possibly be true:

1. All crows are black birds. Not all birds are black.

   A. Not all crows are birds.

   B. All birds are crows.

   C. Not all birds are crows.

   D. Some crows are not black.

   E. Not enough information.

2. No freelancers are employees. All employees are paid benefits.

   A. Some freelancers are paid benefits.

   B. All employees are freelancers.

   C. Some employees are freelancers.

   D. No freelancers are paid benefits.

   E. Not enough information.

3. All doctors are licensed professionals. Some licensed professionals work part-time.

A. Some doctors work part-time.

B. Some licensed professionals are doctors.

C. No doctors work part time.

D. All doctors work part time.

E. Not enough information.

4. No dogs are cats. All cats have 4 legs.

A. No dogs have 4 legs.

B. Some cats are dogs.

C. Some dogs have 4 legs.

D. All dogs have 4 legs.

E. Not enough information.

5. Some underpaid staff went on strike. Some teachers are underpaid staff.

A. All underpaid staff are teachers.

B. All teachers are underpaid staff.

C. Some teachers went on strike.

D. No teachers went on strike.

E. Not enough information.

Answers

These questions are called syllogisms and are often used in IQ tests to measure a person's deductive reasoning skills. The question poses a problem by providing you a major and a minor premise, and then asking you a conclusion based on the information that the premise provides.

This premise is what you might consider your 'general knowledge' from which to deduce smaller bits of information.

1. Major premise: All crows are black birds.

Minor premise: Not all birds are black.

Conclusion: Not all birds are crows. (Option C).

2. Major premise: No freelancers are employees.

Minor premise: All employees are paid benefits.

Conclusion: No freelancers are paid benefits. (Option D).

3. Major premise: All doctors are licensed professionals.

Minor premise: Some licensed professionals work part-time.

Conclusion: Some doctors work part-time.

4. Major premise: No dogs are cats.

Minor premise: All cats have 4 legs.

Conclusion: Not enough information. (Option E). Just because dogs are not cats, doesn't mean they can't have 4 legs.

5. Major premise: Some underpaid staff went on strike.

   Minor premise: Some teachers are underpaid staff.

   Conclusion: Some teachers went on strike. (Option C).

Chapter 7:

Improving Your Inductive Reasoning

"You have been in Afghanistan, I perceive."

"How on earth did you know that?" I asked in astonishment[...]"You were told, no doubt."

"Nothing of the sort. I knew you came from Afghanistan. From long habit the train of thoughts ran so swiftly through my mind, that I arrived at the conclusion without being conscious of intermediate steps.

There were such steps, however. The train of reasoning ran, 'Here is a gentleman of a medical type, but with the air of a military man. Clearly an army doctor, then. He has just come from the tropics, for his face is dark, and that is not the natural tint of his skin, for his wrists are fair. He has undergone hardship and sickness, as his haggard face says clearly. His left arm has been injured. He holds it in a stiff and unnatural manner.'

Where in the tropics could an English army doctor have seen much hardship and got his arm wounded? Clearly in Afghanistan."

- Dialogue between Sherlock Holmes and John Watson, A Study in Scarlet

Many people often confuse deductive reasoning with inductive reasoning, which was potentially Sherlock's most interesting skill. The master detective was popular for his capability to conjure outlandish (however accurate) generalizations based on small pieces of information he would find.

The main difference between inductive and deductive reasoning is that inductive logic *puts small pieces of information together* to arrive at one general concept or truth. Unlike deductive logic which *takes*, inductive logic *adds* things together.

In many ways, inductive reasoning can be harder than deductive reasoning because it requires that we take bits of information to come up with a pattern, a trend, or a general concept. Because there can be a variety of possible patterns to any given situation, it can take more time to figure out how pieces work together to create a bigger picture.

How to Improve Inductive Reasoning Skills
In the quote above, Sherlock shows us just how astounding his inductive logic can be. The dialogue happened during Holmes and Watson's first encounter - a time during which neither man knew

anything about the other. Holmes needed to cut costs on lodgings, which prompted him to seek out a person to share the space and the rent with him. Watson was the man that ultimately took the opportunity.

Prior to the meeting, neither of the men actually knew any in-depth details about one another, especially when it came to their prior engagements and occupation, so, when Sherlock said he presumed that Watson had been in Afghanistan, in a non-inquisitive tone, the good doctor was perplexed. How did this man know? It was Sherlock's inductive reasoning at work.

He observed Watson - from his darkened skin that was uneven with his wrists where perhaps a watch might have shielded it against the sun, to his tired and haggard face, to his seemingly injured arm which was held stiffly against his side. Holmes put these pieces, or clues, together and surmised that Watson had probably come from a place in the tropics where the sun darkened his skin, and where he might have encountered quite some physical hardship and even injurious events.

Where else could that be other than Afghanistan? Remember that the book *A Study in Scarlet* was set in the year 1881 - just one year after the end of the 2nd Anglo-Afghan War.

Sherlock Holmes' inductive reasoning skills were definitely several notches better than many others, but how did he improve the skill through the years? Of course, there's no way to tell, but there are a few widely accepted modern day practices that can help you target your inductive reasoning skills.

1. **Individually, then all at once -** The key to perfecting the skill of inductive logic is by establishing the right method of interpreting data. Remember that the process involves seeing different parts of a whole and figuring out how they fit together. Sherlock only had different aspects of Watson's appearance as his clues, but he was able to add them up to conclude that the doctor had served in

Afghanistan.

In typical IQ and diagnostic tests, inductive logic is tested by way of shapes moving in a pattern. One of the figures in the sequence will be left blank, and the examinee is tasked to fill in the space given the

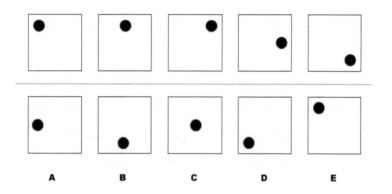

choices provided.

Take this sequence for example. Given the items, what pattern do they create? Given the pattern, what object comes next in the sequence? Based on what's presented, we can see that the black dot in the box moves around in a clockwise pattern, with each corner representing one stop, and each edge representing one stop.

Given this pattern, we can assume that the next item in the sequence should be option B.

Looking at each individual item's qualities will help you pick up on how it relates to the next item in the sequence. What changed, and what remains the same? Comparing item one and item two, we can see that the square shape, as well as the colors and sizes of the elements don't change. What does shift is the position of the dot inside the square.

Once the difference has been established, it's time to determine the trend in that change throughout the sequence. In this example, we see that the black dot moves in a predictable pattern through the space, leading us to conclude the general idea or pattern of the brain exercise.

2. **A Change of Perspective** - Sometimes, when presented with a set of clues or elements, we tend to look at them in a linear pattern because

that's what we're used to but, changing your perspective can help improve the way you perform on inductive reasoning tests.

For instance, if a set of shapes or numbers just aren't making any sense to you, then you can consider looking at them from the end towards the front. Changing your perspective and taking on the problem from a different aspect will allow you to see other aspects of the issue that might not have been apparent at the start.

3. **A Matter of Chance** - A lot of times, Sherlock would take a chance with his inductive logic, sticking to his gut and deciding on a conclusion no matter how farfetched or unlikely it might have seemed. Why? "How often have I said to you that when you have eliminated the impossible, whatever remains, however impossible, must be the truth?" This is one of the super sleuth's most famous lines, and for good reason.

In a lot of ways, inductive reasoning can feel like

guesswork, especially if there's not a lot for you to work with. Some psychometric tests make sure that the trends or patterns in a question are as vague as possible, making it difficult to be exactly sure when it comes to developing a decision.

Take this question for example:

Margaret wore a blue dress and a black hat to work on Monday.

On Tuesday, she wore black slacks, a fuschia blouse, and a mustard hat.

What will she wear on Wednesday?

    A. An orange pantsuit and a pink hat.

    B. A green dress and a purple coat.

It's really not a lot of information to go off of. Is there a trend? Hardly. Two days' worth of wardrobe choices rarely qualifies as substantial information to draw a trend. On top of that, there seems to be no obvious pattern when it comes to her choice of color, so how can you make a decision?

The best possible way to answer the question would be to find even just the slightest general truth and then decide the answer that coincides with it most closely. With that considered, we can say that the best choice would be option A. Now, the question is *why?*

Despite Margaret's clothing choices being widely different, we can see that she wore a hat on both days. That said, it's *more probable* that she would wear a hat on Wednesday than not. Since there are no other trends that can be established, we can *assume* that she would choose to wear a hat.

Some questions are phrased similarly, but ultimately require that you do the same mental work. For example, you're told to reach into a bag of candy 3 times. The bag itself is completely opaque, so there's no way to see its contents. On your first attempt, you draw out your hand and see a mini chocolate bar. On your second attempt, the same chocolate bar. On your third, the same.

Given this information, you might conclude that the

bag of candy contains nothing other than that specific type of chocolate bar. Is it a guaranteed truth? No. Even if there was only 1 other piece of candy in the bag, your conclusion would be wrong. Is it probable though, that the bag only contains that specific type of chocolate bar? Yes, there is a high probability.

In many cases, Sherlock had nothing more to trust than his keen knack for calculating probabilities. While the super sleuth did say that he never 'guessed' (The Sign of Four), he did often make educated and well thought-out conclusions that he would draw from induction.

Learning to become confident in the patterns you discover, no matter how seemingly small or insignificant can lead you on a trail of truth and even bring you closer to the stunning conclusion to a problem.

Honing Your Inner Holmes - DIY Experiment

Inductive reasoning is best measured by way of visual or numerical tests that provide some sort of pattern. Examinees are tasked to determine the pattern based on the provided images and then fill out the blanks to complete the sequence.

Try to determine how these different variables come together to create a trend, and choose the best option to complete the sequence:

1. 2 - 8 - 26 - ___ - 242

    A. 78

    B. 52

    C. 80

    D. 91

2. 5230 - 5131 - 5031 - 4932 - ____ - 4733

    A. 4834

    B. 4791

C. 4880

D. 4832

3. 8 - 64 - 16 - 256 - ___ - 4096

A. 64

B. 72

C. 80

D. 54

Answers

The key to answering inductive logic questions correctly is by taking all the different details (in this case, variables) into account and finding out how they are related to one another. The objective is to establish a pattern or a general truth that the variables follow.

1. Each number is multiplied by 3 and then increased by 2. Given this pattern, the correct option is C.

2. Numbers are reduced alternately by 99 and then 100. The correct option would be D.

3. Variables are squared and divided by 4 alternately. In this case, the correct answer would be option A.

In this next test, you'll be given two phrases that provide some information on a situation. Determine the pattern and choose the answer that best suits the trend you've established.

1. A farmer is trying to figure out the best crops to grow on his land. He has three plots on which to grow three different types of produce. On the first try, he uses the first plot for potatoes, the second for buckwheat, and the third for tomatoes.

After harvesting each type of produce, he moves on to the next types he wants to try and so, on his second attempt, he uses the first plot for watermelons, the second for rice, and the third for melons.

What will he grow on the third attempt?

    A. Carrots, millet, cucumber.

    B. Squash, barley, radish.

2. A woman visits her local hair salon three times a month. On her first visit for the month of January, she gets a haircut, a pedicure, and a foot spa. On her second visit for January, she gets her hair colored. On her third visit, she gets a haircut and a manicure.

Will she get a haircut on her first visit in February?

    A. Yes

    B. No

Answers

1. The most likely answer is A. The farmer is following a pattern which entails that the first plot will be used for produce that grows closely to or in the ground, the second plot

for grains, and the third for fruits.

2. The woman is unlikely to get a haircut on her first visit in February. Given the information, she does not seem to get a haircut on the week following a previous haircut.

Again, none of the answers provided are guaranteed to be true - as with most answers arrived at through inductive logic; however, because these trends are the only ones we can establish given the limited information, the choices made are *most likely to be true*.

Chapter 8:

How To Get A Laser-Focused Mind

"Never trust to general impressions, my boy, but concentrate yourself upon details."

- Sherlock Holmes, The Adventures of Sherlock Holmes

There is no better way to put facts together, clear the mind, and sharpen the tools in your mental arsenal other than meditation. This seemingly simple practice can help you become laser-focused, allowing you to clear away clutter so you can concentrate only on what's most important and relevant.

While Sherlock never truly made mention of meditation, we can infer from the many moments that Watson would catch him zoned out by his desk that he did, in fact, utilize the concept of meditation, although not in the traditional sense. This allowed the super sleuth to refresh his mind, think of new perspectives, and see information in a new light in order to discover new truths and find where other clues might fit in.

On top of allowing Holmes to dissect existing information, meditation also helped him develop a sense of clarity when faced with new mental challenges. The practice *trained his mind* to develop an *investigative* mode which he could turn on and off as he pleased. With this, he was able to readily clear his mind when confronted with a mystery regardless of what he was thinking of moments before.

Meditation is a lot more than just sitting down and closing your eyes. There is a process to the practice, and it does require some cognitive awareness for proper execution.

Meditation for Everyday Life

In our modern day and age, there are millions of individuals who engage in meditation for a variety of reasons - whether it's for reducing stress, refocusing on their goals, or simply for calming down after a hectic day at the office.

Aside from helping people calm the senses, however, meditation can also be used to sharpen the mind. Clearing your head of mental clutter every so often can help make your thought process more efficient. This has also been said to be beneficial in terms of coming up with the right decisions, especially if you're confronted with a particularly confusing situation.

How can you effectively use meditation to optimize the way you make decisions in your everyday life? Consider these tips:

1. **Make sure you're comfortable** - Just like good ol' Sherlock, you don't necessarily need to follow the traditional posture that people have been using for

meditation. Sitting on the floor with your legs crossed for extended periods of time can actually be very straining on the back and the tailbone.

When it comes to meditation, comfort is of the utmost importance. Any sort of pain or discomfort that you might experience could have an effect on the quality of your meditation as pain takes up space in your mental bandwidth. Having as little stimulation on your body as possible will help make the entire process far more fulfilling.

Instead of trying to do it as the traditionalists do though, you can do it like Sherlock and find a position that works for you. Your favorite chair, a spot on your bed, or even a cozy little nook outdoors can all be great alternatives, depending on what you prefer.

As for closing your eyes, it's entirely up to you. Some people can focus on their cognition better when there isn't any visual stimulation, and others are the exact opposite. The same goes for your hands.

For instance, some people feel more comfortable twiddling since it works as a psychomotor outlet that improves the intensity of concentration. This often works best for people who feel that sitting or standing still for too long might be unnatural or too effortful.

2. **Silent, but not too silent** - Some people tend to think that the ideal atmosphere for meditation is one of absolute silence, but that's not always the case. In fact, some **studies** have found that mild auditory stimulation can help fire up the brain and make it far more efficient than if it were being prompted in an unnaturally quiet environment.

Remember that we rarely ever find ourselves in absolute silence, so your mind will be better adjusted to *some* sound than none at all. That said, you might want to consider playing some quiet tunes while you meditate.

Calming songs, classical music, or even simple ambient music mimicking the great outdoors can be beneficial if you're trying to improve the outcomes of your meditation practice.

3. **Aim for effortless** - A common mistake people make when trying to meditate is focusing too hard to achieve that quiet mental state. Forcing your mind into a state of **rumination** can be counterintuitive, causing you to exert more effort on trying to achieve silence and preventing you from thinking about more important matters.

As a general rule, you should be more interested in allowing your mind to wander and flow into mindfulness, rather than forcing it. After finding the right spot, setting the mood, and finding the most comfortable positioning for your meditation session, try not to force your mind into thinking.

Instead, let ideas flow and slowly guide your mind towards the situation you want to address. Allowing your mind to wander, instead of pressuring it into thinking, can make the entire process far more beneficial.

Honing Your Inner Holmes - DIY Exercise

Improving the way you meditate can unlock untapped cognitive skills and sharpen the tools in your mental arsenal. Even a few minutes every day can make a grand difference in the way your thought process works, so it's ideal that you dedicate some time to meditation on a routine schedule.

Consider these tips to set up a fool-proof meditation

practice.

1. Find the best time in your day when you are most available to meditate without distractions. This can be different times every day as long as it is free from interruptions. Some prefer meditating first thing in the morning, while others schedule their practice before going to bed.

2. Set an alarm for your meditation practice so you don't forget when to start. It's important that you allow a few minutes of preparation, so make sure to set your alarm slightly ahead of your intended hour of meditation.

3. Designate a concept or idea to your meditation practice. Others choose setting a weekly topic, such as family, relationships, finance, or work which will be the central focus of the meditation practice throughout the entire week.

4. Try downloading guided meditation audio files to help ease you into the practice if you're unsure what to do. These guides provide you with the general direction to help your thoughts flow if you feel that you're not quite confident enough to tackle meditation independently.

Post-Meditation Worksheet

Fill out the table based on your experience with your meditation practice. Feel free to write or draw your answers depending on what you deem fit.

Cognitive Tasks
What ideas, concepts, or thoughts did you dwell on during this session? What were you hoping to achieve in today's practice?

Revelations or Conclusions

What truths were you able to discover through your meditation?

Practical Application

How can you use these revelations or conclusions in your everyday life?

Chapter 9:

Metacognition: Sharpen The Saw

"You know my methods. Apply them."

- Sherlock Holmes, The Sign of Four

You can think of metacognition as a stone on which to sharpen the rest of your mental tools. The process of metacognition lets you *think* about the way you *think*, allowing you to pick up any errors in your methods and enhancing or optimizing it to get the best results out of your efforts.

Metacognition is an essential aspect of improving the way you use your knowledge, logic, skills, and characteristics so that your thinking process produces accurate, reliable, and relevant outcomes each time. The more you *think* about how you *think*, the faster, more efficient, and perhaps even the smarter you'll become.

Consider this scenario: A skilled physicist and a student are given the same problem - solving the amount of water lost from a tank given that a single drop of water drips every N seconds. To start, each one is given a basic solution with which to work with.

Both the physicist and the student get the right answer for the first question, and are handed a second question to solve. While this next problem is similar to the first, many of the variables have changed, and an added aspect of water dripping *into* the tank is included as another variable.

The student uses the same solution, not knowing that the added variable calls for a change in the approach, while the physicist alters his technique in order to accommodate the different factors that have been tweaked in the second problem.

The difference between the two is that in this particular subject matter, the physicist *knew* that a shift in process was necessary, which is why he *thought* about the way he had solved the first problem and discovered that it wasn't a sound solution for the second. Metacognition played a role in his capability to detect that the previous methods were going to be ineffective the second time around.

Unfortunately, the student wasn't as well aware of this factor and ended up using the same method despite the obvious change in the variables and the problem itself.

The Development of Metathinking

Because it is such an abstract concept, it's not that easy to truly grasp how it's done. For everyone, it can be different, especially because not every person *thinks* the same way; however, there are some general practices that have been found to benefit most people when it comes to improving their thought process through metacognition.

1. **Knowing What You Know** - It's been said time and time again that *what you don't know can't hurt you, but,* anyone who wants to think more like Holmes

needs to understand that it definitely can. The same goes for the concept that *ignorance is bliss*.

Knowing what you know, and knowing that there are things you *don't* know, will help you understand what you need to learn in order to bridge the gaps in your knowledge. Philosophical in nature, this aspect of metacognition was widely used throughout ancient philosophy by icons like Plato, and in 17th century philosophy by experts like John Locke.

The concept itself is called epistemology, and it deals with knowledge, particularly its method, validity, and scope. The objective of epistemology is to determine between justified fact or truth, and mere opinion.

Of course, ask anyone *if* they know what they know, and they're likely to respond with a confident 'yes', but there's a lot more to *knowing* than simply *believing* that you know.

Consider this: You have boarded a plane with a close friend. At 28,000 feet above sea level, you both take a glance over the vast expanse below you. "What beautiful, sea foam green waters" you sigh gently. Indeed, the Caspian Sea looked particularly lively today.

"You mean beautiful sapphire blue waters?" your friend points out. You take another glance and think to yourself, *"No, that's definitely sea foam green."* You shrug and rest your back against your seat.

"It's a little too cold for comfort in here" you whisper, as you throw on a scarf. "I think it's just right" responds your friend who happened to be wearing a jacket over his shirt. You call on the stewardess and ask for a hot cup of coffee.

The plane lands and you make your way

through the airport, claim your bags, and contact a ride to your hotel. As you step out, you both feel the sudden warmth of the outdoors as cars and city buses pass you by. "I didn't think it would be this hot here!" you giggle to your friend. He smiles back as he starts to remove his jacket.

"Consider yourselves lucky," a friendly local standing nearby interjects, "This is one of the cooler days we've had in the past few months."

In this scenario, there are 3 truths that were all fact based on how you perceived them - the color of the Caspian, the cold temperature in the cabin, and the warmth outdoors. These were 3 'realities' that you *knew*.

However, these 3 'facts' were challenged by others around you - when you friend said the sea was sapphire blue, when he claimed that the temperature in the cabin was just right, and when the local outside said that it was a cool day.

Given these interactions now, how can you be *certain* that what you *know* is fact and not mere opinion? It can definitely be flustering, but this is the purpose of epistemology. Many of us rely on what our senses perceives, which can often be flawed or laced with bias. This can cloud our judgment and prevent us from *knowing* things as they truly are.

Sherlock would often talk about thinking without bias, and the investigator was careful to make sure that these biases did not exist, not only when it came to his ideas, but also in terms of how he perceived evidence. That's why he would often close his eyes when piecing together information, as this helped him concentrate on what was true without the influence of egocentric tendencies.

2. **Creating Schemata** - Immanuel Kant was the one who first introduced the concept of schema or schemata. This concept involves creating a mental diagram in order to connect concepts and ideas in order to develop a general concept.

Of course, Kant's Critique of Pure Reason goes much deeper than most of us can comprehend, but what we can take away from his use of the schema is that *organizing information* into categories in our minds can help bring new truths to light.

Consider this example: You've discovered that the hidden safe in your office had been opened and its content stolen; however, only half of the value kept inside the safe was taken. Unfortunately, the security cameras in your office were turned off when the incident occurred. You inspect the safe and find that it hadn't been broken, but was instead opened using the combination.

Given this information, you create a mental diagram of the details you currently know to be true.

You consider the different aspects of the situation

and try to use inductive reasoning to try to come up with more information. You know for a fact that there are only 2 other people who know the combination to your safe - your assistant and your wife, so you narrow down your suspects to these 2 individuals, assuming they told no-one else about the combination.

You consider the fact that the theft was executed when the cameras were turned off - a routine that is observed regularly from 5pm to 8am the next day when your office is closed. This means that the person responsible was aware that this would be a safe time to commit the theft because they knew the cameras would be switched off.

Then, you consider the amount that was taken. There was a total of $10,500 USD in cash in the safe, among other valuable items including jewelry and land titles, but the perpetrator only took around $4,000 USD in cash and left everything else untouched. You remember your assistant talking about his mother's medical bills which their family was struggling to afford.

With this new information, you expand your diagram further.

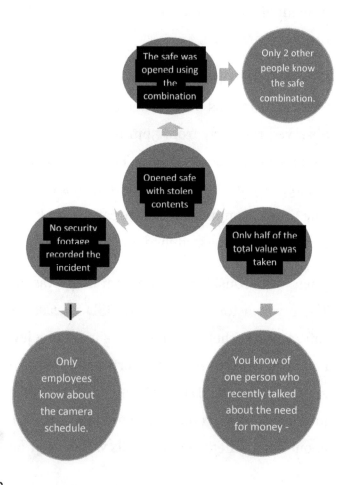

Now, with this expanded schema, you have a clearer understanding of how all the information comes together. The secondary aspects of the concept can actually be further interconnected. For instance, the fact that only employees are aware of the camera schedule in your office already gives away the truth that the perpetrator could not have been your wife since she isn't one of your employees.

Knowing that your assistant was vocal about his need for cash and that he was the only other person aware of the combination, aside from your wife, makes it probable that he was responsible for the theft.

While we might not know it, we actually create new schemata and add to old ones every day. However, consciously using this method is a great way to exercise metacognition because it organizes thoughts and ideas, putting them into a clear perspective, and establishes how each piece of information relates with another.

1. **Asking Questions** – It is one thing to ask questions to learn new information, and another thing to ask questions to shape your own thinking. Auditing your mental process will help bring certain errors to light, and will establish an awareness of how you can make your thinking more efficient.

Here are a few examples of questions you can ask to become a better thinker:

- *What proves that this information is correct?*

- *What are my reasons for thinking this way?*

- *Are there any fallacies in the way that I've reasoned this out?*

- *Am I choosing this because it benefits me/my goal?*

- *Have I involved my emotions in this decision?*

- *Have I done this before? If I have, were*

there poor outcomes from the last time I tried this?

The purpose of asking these questions is to eliminate bias and show where your train of thought might be directed. Stopping it in its tracks and figuring out whether there were other directions that you could possibly explore will make it possible to see the entire truth.

When formulating questions to sharpen your mental skills, try to think of queries that will target your cognitive process. Asking about the way you think, instead of asking what you think, can be far more beneficial when it comes to shaping your mental arsenal for clearer, sharper functioning.

2. **Verbalizing Information** - Studies that date back as far as the 60s have concluded that verbalizing our thoughts can help monumentally when it comes to our mental process. But how? Some experts say that verbalization allows us to slow down our thinking, and observe the problem more

deliberately.

This heightened consciousness of the issue and the elements surrounding it lets you zoom out, see the entire problem as one big picture, and thus allows you to develop the ideal *process* to tackle the situation.

You can think of it like a maze - if you're standing right smack in the middle, you won't be able to see the different paths and where they lead. Any turns you take will be guided purely by your knowledge of where you have already been but, if you can zoom out and see the maze as a whole, then you can map out the direction you should go in order to escape.

When verbalizing your thoughts on a problem, it's not entirely necessary to have someone listening; however, Holmes never complained that Watson was around to hear him out. Just saying things loudly, clearly, and deliberately will allow you to establish a more concrete grasp of the situation, as well as develop a suitable plan to escape.

Honing Your Inner Holmes - DIY Experiment

There are times in the past when you have probably used metacognition without you knowing. These are instances when you might have made an obvious or significant error, and you made a firm resolve to avoid making the same mistakes again in the future.

Try to complete this short exercise to find out when you might have used metacognition in the past.

QUESTION	EXAMPLE	ANSWER
Describe a past event or instance when you learned that you made a verified mistake.	*I arrived at my hospital shift wearing the wrong color-coded scrubs designated for that specific day.*	
Why did you think you were doing the right thing prior to learning of the	*I believed it was a Wednesday because it was the same day my*	

error?	*electricity bill arrived. The bill usually arrives on Wednesdays, but may actually arrive any day of the week.*	
What was wrong with your original pattern of thinking?	*I based my work clothes schedule on an event that 'usually' happened on a specific day, but was actually not a reliable marker since it was subject to change.*	
How did you correct this thought process to make sure the problem never happened again?	*I designed a conspicuous color-coded schedule that I posted on my bedroom wall. I also made sure to place my previous uniform on top of the hamper to remind myself what color I wore yesterday.*	

Seeing how you applied metacognitive tactics in the past allows you to understand how they can be applied in the future. Auditing the way these past changes have improved your current situation, or have mitigated risks and errors, can also shed light on what you can do now to address any issues that you currently struggle with.

Now, ask yourself - when have I applied metacognition to my daily practices? What are the current issues, problems, or struggles I have with everyday life? How can I improve the way I handle these challenges? Does it have anything to do with the way I've been letting my cognition work?

Often, you'll find the best application for metacognition by inspecting the difficulties of your life more closely. Challenges with your finances, relationships, work life, or school life are all feasibly starting points to try to use the process of *thinking about thinking*.

Conclusion

"I cannot live without brainwork. What else is there to live for? Stand at the window here. Was ever such a dreary, dismal, unprofitable world? See how the yellow fog swirls down the street and drifts across the duncolored houses. What could be more hopelessly prosaic and material?"

- Sherlock Holmes, The Complete Sherlock Holmes Vol. 1

Despite being an intelligent, capable, and skilled physician, Dr. Arthur Conan Doyle was best known for creating Sherlock Holmes - perhaps the most iconic character in investigative fiction up to our present day. In fact, Doyle has been more recognized for his award-winning character than for his medical work - a telling sign of just how a transcendent genius Sherlock Holmes was.

Throughout the years, countless other fictional characters have been patterned after the super sleuth legend, including the popular drama series doctor, Gregory House. In recent interviews, the creators of this medical series admitted that the character was heavily modeled after the great Sherlock - from his antisocial demeanor, knack for brainwork, rejection of 'boring' cases, and even down to his name. In entertainment history, there is no other fictional human character that has been filmed more than Sherlock Holmes, starring in a total of 226 films since the advent of cinema.

Needless to say, the master detective has become a worldwide phenomenon, not only because he astounds with his incredible prowess for detective work, but because he shows us just *how powerful* the human mind can be.

Although Holmes is a fictional character, the way that Conan Doyle fashioned his persona made it so that he would be a *realistic* character nonetheless, and his cognitive capabilities, albeit uncommon, *can be attained* with training and practice.

These days, countless people from around the globe

have tried to emulate Sherlock, reading the books, watching the shows, and immersing themselves in the great literary works and film productions that showcase the man's unprecedented mental skills.

If you've been paying attention all this time, this guide should have helped you sharpen the tools in your mental arsenal to help shape your thought process to resemble Sherlock's.

Remember that according to research, we only use about 20% of our brain's capacity, so while this book might have helped you unlock more potential, there is a vast ocean of cognitive capability that's untapped and waiting to be used - and it's up to you to unlock them.

So, as the master detective himself would have said, *"You know my methods. Apply them."*

Finally, if you enjoyed this book, then I'd like to ask you for a favor. Would you be kind enough to leave a review for this book on Amazon?

It'd be greatly appreciated!

Thank you and good luck!